FREEDOM
INSIDE
THE
ORGANIZATION

FREEDOM INSIDE THE ORGANIZATION

Bringing Civil Liberties to the Workplace

David W. Ewing

A Sunrise Book
E. P. DUTTON
New York

Library of Congress Cataloging in Publication Data

Ewing, David W
    Freedom inside the organization.

    "A Sunrise book."
    1. Employee rights—United States.   I.   Title.
HD8072.E94   1977   323.4   77-498

    ISBN: 0-87690-249-2

Published simultaneously in Canada by Clarke, Irwin & Company
Limited, Toronto and Vancouver

10 9 8 7 6 5 4 3 2 1

First Edition

To E., B., S., and R.

CONTENTS

vii

PREFACE

This book did not grow out of a master plan, in the way a well-designed house or factory is built. Rather, it began as a one-room cabin, was expanded to several rooms and a second story, and then was connected with other cabins. The resulting structure is sufficient as a shelter for some ideas that I think are important, but it is hardly more than that. Already I sense that the ideas are bursting to move into newer and better housing.

About a decade ago some leading businessmen asked me questions as an editor that I could not answer. The businessmen were looking for articles and books that might shed light on problems of justice in organizations—not so much pay, safety, or working conditions as matters like "due process" and "rights."

Unable to refer my correspondents to publications of the sort they wanted, I began studying the subject myself. One survey grew into several surveys, one newspaper article grew into a series, a short article for one magazine grew into a longer article for another magazine, and the various fragmented efforts together grew into this volume.

None of these expansions could be planned in advance. Each was encouraged by readers and listeners who indicated there was more, much more, to be said about a vast subject that we scarcely have a name for yet. Some called it "employee rights." Others referred to it as "due process" or "constitutionalism." Some people used such descriptions as "puppets" and "autocrats." The semantic difficulties did not deter us. What we wanted to discuss and make room for had reality even if it lacked an agreed-on label.

For enormous amounts of typing, correspondence, checking, and other help, I am indebted to Patricia J. S. Weaver. In addition, I want to thank the Harvard Business School and *Harvard Business Review* for enabling me to take an extra month of free time in the 1975–1976 academic year under a University regulation concerning twenty-five-year employees. This "bonus" helped greatly in completing the manuscript.

The opinions and conclusions expressed in this volume are, of course, my own and do not necessarily reflect the thinking of others at the Harvard Business School.

D.W.E.

Winchester, Massachusetts

PART I

Introduction

Let me add that a bill of rights is what the
people are entitled to against every government
on earth, general or particular. . . .

> —Thomas Jefferson, letter
> of December 20, 1787 to
> James Madison

1

THE
BLACK HOLE
IN
AMERICAN RIGHTS

For nearly two centuries Americans have enjoyed freedom of press, speech, and assembly, due process of law, privacy, freedom of conscience, and other important rights—in their homes, churches, political forums, and social and cultural life. But Americans have not enjoyed these civil liberties in most companies, government agencies, and other organizations where they work. Once a U.S. citizen steps through the plant or office door at 9 A.M., he or she is nearly rightless until 5 P.M., Monday through Friday. The employee continues to have political freedoms, of course, but these are not the significant ones now. While at work, the important relationships are with bosses, associates, and subordinates. Inequalities in dealing with these people are what really count for an employee.

To this generalization there are important exceptions. In some organizations, generous managements have seen fit to assure free speech, privacy, due process, and other concerns as privileges. But there is no guarantee the privileges will survive the next change of chief executive. As former Attorney General Ramsey Clark once said in a speech, "A right is not what someone gives you; it's what no one can take from you." Defined in this manner, rights are rare in business and public organizations.

3

Rightlessness is most conspicuous for employees who do not belong to unions—for most engineers, scientists, technicians, accountants, sales people, secretaries, managers, administrative assistants, and people in related categories. These nonunionized employees make up the great majority of nongovernment workers—about 50 million of the 72 million total. A comment once made by a middle manager applies to all. "When I first came here," the manager said, referring to the corporation that employed him, "I was given a book which said 'Welcome' on the cover and, inside, spelled out my duties and obligations . . . they took up about 15 pages. My rights numbered two: A share in the company's insurance plan and a two-week vacation every year. They took up about 15 lines."[1]

Union members are not much better off, as a rule. In later chapters we shall note some significant exceptions, where union Robin Hoods bounded to the aid of employees penalized for speaking out or resisting an unethical directive. But in general the unions seem to have been far more interested in the material conditions of work life—pay, hours, safety, cleanliness, seniority—than in civil liberties. In fact, these powerful bureaucracies seem to be not much different from the corporate organizations they joust with as far as employee rights are concerned.

What about government? Here there is a little more light but not much. A series of federal court decisions beginning in 1968 appears to have removed the gag from many public employees, but as yet few civil servants have paid much attention to these decisions on speech, or even know about them. As for such other rights as privacy, due process, and conscience, government employees are in the same ghetto as corporate employees.

In recent years the press has noted numerous casualties of free speech in the Pentagon, Food and Drug Administration, Atomic Energy Commission, and other federal agencies, as well as in state and city governments. Occasionally an especially determined dissident will return in triumph, as A. Ernest Fitzgerald, a Pentagon employee, did after testifying against his superiors' wishes about cost overruns on the Lockheed C5A. But most of the dissidents have been buried, and it is as sure as turnips and taxes that for every casualty reported, countless others have gone unreported. Only because of the valiant efforts of a Senator William Proxmire here and a Senator Edward Kennedy there, and the limited efforts of the Civil Service to rescue abused employees, do people in government agencies fare a little better than people in tightly controlled private corporations.

What about other types of organizations, such as colleges and universities, professional firms, research agencies, and health organizations? In general, they seem to follow the same practices as business and government. In a few progressive organizations privileges are enjoyed—the autocracy is benevolent. But the organization is still an autocracy.

In effect, therefore, U.S. society is a paradox. The Constitution and Bill of Rights light up the sky over political campaigners, legislators, civic leaders, families, church people, and artists. But not so over employees. The employee sector of our civil liberties universe is more like a black hole, with rights so compacted, so imploded by the gravitational forces of legal tradition, that, like the giant black stars in the physical universe, light can scarcely escape.

Perhaps the most ironic thing is that only in recent years have Americans made many noises about this paradox. It is as if we took it for granted and assumed there was no alternative. "Organizations have always been this way and always have to be," we seem to say. One is reminded of an observation attributed to Marshall McLuhan: "Anybody's total surround, or environment, creates a condition of nonperception."

To put the situation in focus, let us make a brief review of rights in the workplace.

Speech. In many private and public organizations there is a well-oiled machinery for providing relief to an employee who is discharged because of his or her race, religion, or sex. But we have no mechanisms for granting similar relief to an employee who is discharged for exercising the right of free speech. The law states that all employers "may dismiss their employees at will . . . for good cause, for no cause, or even for cause morally wrong, without being thereby guilty of legal wrong."[2]

Of course, discharge is only the extreme weapon; many steps short of discharge may work well enough—loss of a raise in pay, demotion, assignment to the boondocks, or perhaps simply a cutback of normal and expected benefits.

Consider the case of a thirty-five-year-old business executive whom I shall call "Mike Z." He was a respected research manager in a large company. He believed that his company was making only superficial efforts to comply with newly enacted pollution laws. In a management meeting and later in social groups he spoke critically of top management's attitude. Soon strange things began to happen to him, different only in degree from what happens to a political dissenter in the Soviet Union. First, his place in the company parking lot was canceled. Then his name was "accidentally" removed from the office building directory inside the main entrance. Soon routine requests he made to attend professional meetings began to get snarled up in red tape or were "lost." Next he found himself harassed by directives to rewrite routine reports. Then his budget for clerical service was cut, followed by a drastic slash in his research budget. When he tried to protest this treatment, he met a wall of top management silence. Rather than see his staff suffer further for his dissidence, he quit his job and moved his family to another city.

Mike Z. could be almost anyone in thousands of companies, government agencies, and other organizations. It should not be surprising, therefore, that when it comes to speaking out on issues of company policy or management practice, employees make about as much noise as fish swimming.

So well-established is the idea that any criticism of the company is "ratting" or "finking" that some companies hang out written prohibitions for all to see. For instance, a private bus company on the West Coast puts employees on notice with this rule:

> The company requires its employees to be loyal. It will not tolerate words or acts of hostility to the company, its officers, agents, or employees, its services, equipment or its condition, or . . . criticisms of the company to others than . . . superior officers.

In 1971 the bus company fired a driver who had become so frustrated over the repeated mechanical failures, worn tires, defective brakes, and smoking exhausts of the vehicles he operated that he had aired his complaints on a local TV station (he had complained first to his superiors but got no response). The California attorney general's office said it could do nothing to protect the driver, although it regarded the company loyalty rule as unfair. The state's Public Utility Commission also said it could not protect the employee, even though it was concerned with unsafe bus equipment. Only pressure by the union and the TV station succeeded in getting the driver reinstated.[3]

Except for organizations where there are union newspapers and journals there is no freedom of press in American organizations. In the corporate earth here and there an underground press survives. Reportedly, such publications as *AT&T Express, The Stranded Oiler*, (Standard Oil Company of California), and the now-expired *Met Lifer* (Metropolitan Life Insurance Company) have sought to expose racist and sexist company policies as well as alleged violations of the law. An underground newsletter at the U.S. Department of Housing and Urban Development tunnels to the surface of public attention sometimes.

The circulation of underground journals has been low, their publication frequency sporadic, and their editorial quality seedy. Yet the threat of management retaliation is omnipresent and their editors remain anonymous in order to survive. Several years ago a reporter, seeking to find out what it was like to be involved with such a publication, stood in front of Standard Oil's Market Street headquarters in San Francisco and sold copies of *The Stranded Oiler*. After a while, he recounted, an office worker warned him he was being photographed. "Sure enough, at the top of the steps were two hefty men in dark green trench coats, trying to look inconspicuous by pointing their cameras at potted tulips. Another company security agent had his camera tucked under his jacket, with his partner acting as a lookout. A fifth dick rushed past me, camera in hand, jumped into a waiting taxi, and sped off. As in an old Bogart film, I tried to strike up a conversation with a trio of gumshoes who had been standing, eyeing me for twenty minutes, but they denied working for Standard."[4]

Conscientious objection. There is very little protection in industry for employees who object to carrying out immoral, unethical, or illegal orders from their superiors. If the employee doesn't like what he or she is asked to do, the remedy is to pack up and leave. This remedy seems to presuppose an ideal economy, where there is another company down the street with openings for jobs just like the one the employee left. But what about the real world? Here resignation may mean having to uproot one's family and move to a strange city in another state. Or it may mean, for an employee in the semifinals of a career, or for an employee with a specialized competence, not being able to find another suitable job anywhere.

In 1970 Shirley Zinman served as a secretary in a Philadelphia employment agency called LIB Services. One day she was instructed by her bosses to record all telephone conversations she might have with prospective clients. This was to be done for "training purposes," she was told, although the callers were not to be told that their words were being taped. The office manager would monitor the conversations on an extension in her office. Ms. Zinman refused to play along with this game, not only because it was unethical, in her view, but illegal as well—the telephone company's regulations forbade such unannounced telephone recordings.

So Ms. Zinman had to resign. She sought unemployment compensation. The state unemployment pay board refused her application. It reasoned that her resignation was not "compelling and necessitous." With the help of attorneys from the American Civil Liberties Union, she appealed her case to the Pennsylvania Commonwealth Court. In a ruling hailed by civil rights leaders, the court in 1973 reversed the pay board and held that Ms. Zinman was entitled to unemployment compensation because her objection to the unethical directive was indeed a "compelling" reason to quit her job.[5]

What this interesting case leaves unsaid is as important as what it does say: Resignation continues to be the accepted response for the objecting employee. The Pennsylvania court took a bold step in favor of employee rights, for prior to this decision there was little reason to think that the Shirley Zinmans of industry could expect any help at all from the outside world. But within the organization itself, an employee is expected to sit at the feet of the boss's conscience.

Security and privacy. When employees are in their homes, before and after working hours, they enjoy well-established rights to privacy and to protection from arbitrary search and seizure of their papers and possessions. But no such rights protect them in the average company, government agency, or other organization; their superiors need only the flimsiest pretext to search their lockers, desks, and files. The boss can rummage through an employee's letters, memoranda, and tapes looking for evidence that (let us say) he or she is about to "rat" on the company. "Ratting" might include reporting a violation of safety standards to the Occupational Safety and Health Administration (which is provided for by law), or telling Ralph Nader about a product defect, or giving the mayor's office requested information about a violation of energy-use regulations.

It doesn't matter that employees may be right about the facts, or that it may be the superiors, not the employees, who are disloyal to the stockholders. In one of his verses for "The Watergate Mother Goose," published in the *Chicago*

Tribune, Bob Cromie expressed the management rationale as follows:

> I do not like thee, Dr. Fell,
> But why this is I cannot tell;
> Meanwhile, to erase those smiles,
> We plan to rummage thru your files.[6]

Choice of outside activities and associations. In practice, most business employees enjoy no right to work after hours for the political, social, and community organizations of their choice. To be sure, in many companies an enlightened management will encourage as much diversity of choice in outside activities as employees can make. As noted earlier, however, this is an indulgence which can disappear any time, for most states do not mandate such rights, and even in those that do, the rights are poorly protected. An employee who gets fired for his or her choice of outside activities can expect no damages for his loss even if he or she wins a suit against the employer. The employee may only "secure the slight satisfaction of seeing his employer suffer the statutory penalties."[7]

Ironically, however, a company cannot discriminate against people whose politics it dislikes when it *hires* them.[8] It has to wait a few days before it can exercise its prerogatives.

In the federal government, freedom of choice of outside activities seems to be well recognized.

Due process. "Accidents will occur in the best-regulated families," said Mr. Micawber in *David Copperfield.* Similarly, accidents of administration occur even in the best-managed companies, with neurotic, inept, or distracted supervisors inflicting needless harm on subordinates. Many a subordinate who goes to such a boss to protest would be well-advised to keep one foot in the stirrups, for he is likely to be shown to the open country for his efforts.

This generalization does not hold for civil service employees in the federal government, who can resort to a grievance process. Nor does it hold for unionized companies, which also have grievance procedures. But it holds for *most* other organizations. In a later chapter, we shall see that a few organizations voluntarily have established a mechanism to ensure due process.

The absence of a right to due process is especially painful because it is the second element of constitutionalism in organizations. As we shall think of it in this book, employee constitutionalism consists of a set of clearly defined rights, and a means of protecting employees from discharge, demotion, or other penalities imposed when they assert their rights.

MAXI-ROLES OF MINIGOVERNMENTS

Why bother about rightlessness in corporations, government agencies, and other organizations? They are much smaller than state and federal governments, are they not? Must an organization that "rules" an employee only for forty or so hours per week be treated as a government?

For one answer, let us turn to the Founding Fathers. Of course, they did not know or conceive of the modern corporation and public agency, so we cannot read what their thoughts about all this might have been. Perhaps we can make a reasonable guess, however, by comparing some numbers.

If the original thirteen colonies were large and powerful enough to concern the Founding Fathers, it seems likely that those men, if here today, would want to extend their philosophy to other assemblages of equivalent size and magnitude. In the writings of James Madison, Thomas Jefferson, George Mason, Jonas Phillips, Richard Henry Lee, Elbridge Gerry, Luther Martin, and others, there is no inference that human rights were seen as a good thing only some of the time or for some places. Instead, the Fathers saw rights as a universal need.[9]

In 1776, and in 1789, when the Bill of Rights (first ten amendments to the Constitution) was passed by Congress and sent to the states for ratification, trading companies and government agencies were tiny organizations incapable of harboring bureaucracy. Indeed, to use Mr. Micawber's phrase, there was hardly room in them to swing a cat, much less create layer on layer of hierarchy and wall after wall of departmental structure.

Today all that has changed. Some of our corporate and public organizations have larger "populations" than did the thirteen colonies. And a truly vast number of organizations have large enough "populations" to rank as real powers in people's everyday lives. For instance:

—AT&T has more than 939,000 employees, nearly twice the size of the largest colony, Virginia, which had about 493,000 inhabitants in 1776. (See Table 1.)

TABLE 1. COMPARATIVE "POPULATIONS"

A. The 13 Colonies in 1776

Virginia	493,000
Pennsylvania	284,000
Massachusetts	252,000
North Carolina	234,000
Maryland	225,000
Connecticut	196,000
New York	187,000
South Carolina	163,000
New Jersey	129,000
New Hampshire	75,000
Rhode Island	55,000
Georgia	43,000
Delaware	41,400

Source: Albert W. Niemi, Jr., *U.S. Economic History* (Chicago: Rand McNally College Publishing Co., 1975), p. 29. The population figures for 1776 are interpolated from the figures for 1770 and 1780.

B. The 13 Largest Corporate Employers, 1976
(figures rounded)

American Telephone & Telegraph	939,100
General Motors	681,000
Sears, Roebuck	417,000
Ford Motor	416,000
International Telephone & Telegraph	376,000
General Electric	375,000
International Business Machines	288,600
Chrysler	217,600
Woolworth	202,400
General Telephone & Electronics	187,200
J. C. Penney	186,000
U.S. Steel	172,800
Westinghouse Electric	166,000

Source: Fortune, May 1976, pp. 210 ff., for industrials; *Forbes,* May 15, 1976, pp. 186 ff., for nonindustrials.

C. The 13 Largest Federal Agency Employers
(Excluding the Military), 1976

Postal Service	696,100
Veterans Administration	212,100
Health, Education & Welfare	144,900
Treasury	129,000
Agriculture	112,600
Transportation	73,000
Interior	78,400
Justice	50,500
General Services Administration	39,300
Commerce	36,600
State	30,800
Tennessee Valley Authority	28,300
National Aeronautics and Space Administration	25,600

Source: The CBS News Almanac, 1976, p. 148.

—General Motors, with 681,000 employees, is nearly two and one-half times the size of the second largest colony, Pennsylvania, which had a population of about 284,000 people in 1776.

—Westinghouse, the thirteenth largest corporate employer today with 166,000 employees, is four times the size of the thirteenth largest colony, Delaware, which had a population of 41,400. Westinghouse's "population" is also larger than that in 1776 of South Carolina, New Jersey, New Hampshire, Rhode Island, and Georgia.

—Turning to government agencies, the U.S. Postal Service, with 696,000 employees, is far larger than any of the thirteen colonies in 1776. The Veterans Administration, Department of Health, Education, and Welfare, Treasury Department, and Department of Agriculture are all larger than the populations of Delaware, Georgia, Rhode Island, and New Hampshire at the time the Declaration was signed. (See Table 1.)

In fact, 125 corporations have larger "populations" than did Delaware, the smallest colony, in 1776. These corporations range from manufacturers like Singer and Sperry Rand to chemical concerns like Dow and Du Pont, food producers like Beatrice and Borden, retailers like Kresge and Kroger, defense contractors like Litton and Lockheed, and alphabet mixers like CPC and FMC. As for the federal government, eight agencies, in addition to the military, are larger than colonial Georgia and Delaware; three more agencies are close to them in size. (I exclude the Department of Defense, with 1,035,000 employees, from this discussion because of its noncivilian nature.)

Table 1 also shows that the six largest corporate employers alone have a total "population" larger than that of all the thirteen states combined two centuries ago.

But can employee workforces legitimately be compared with state populations? Of course, there are important differences—the twenty-four-hours-per-day jurisdiction of the state as opposed to only eight hours per day for an employer, the fact that the state has courts and military forces while the employer does not, and others. Yet it is not an apples-and-oranges comparison. Decades ago, and long before corporations and public agencies achieved anything like their current size, political scientists were noting many important similarities between the governments of organizations and political governments. In 1908, for example, Arthur Bentley wrote:

> A corporation is government through and through. . . . Certain technical methods which political government uses, as, for instance, hanging, are not used by corporations, generally speaking, but that is a detail.[10]

In numerous ways, sizable corporations, public agencies, and university administrations qualify as "minigovernments." They pay salaries and costs. They have medical plans. They provide for retirement income. They offer recreational facilities. They maintain cafeterias. They may assist an employee with housing, educational loans, personal training, and vacation plans. They schedule numerous social functions. They have "laws," conduct codes, and other rules. Many, as we shall see in a later chapter, have mechanisms for resolving disputes. A few even keep chaplains on the payroll or maintain facilities for religious worship.

Indeed, just to walk around the enormous 3M Company in St. Paul, with its many great buildings, yards, and roads, is to see facilities for nearly all the functions that any state or federal government maintains. The same can be said for American Telephone & Telegraph Company, the Veterans Administration, and any number of other organizations.

In Florida's state university system, there are seven levels of administration over the teaching profession. The upper six of these levels are occupied by "professional administrators," that is, people whose careers are mostly managerial rather than academic. This heavy emphasis on administration shows how important and time-consuming governance has become even in parts of the once unstructured world of academic spirits.

In some ways, the minigovernments of today have closer control over an employee than any state did when the Bill of Rights was enacted in George Washington's first term as president. Most employees work at close quarters under careful supervision. Their work and talk may be monitored, and in any event their performance is measured qualitatively and quantitatively. On the other hand, two centuries ago many Virginians, Pennsylvanians, New Yorkers, and other colonists lived off in the woods and fields somewhere, seeing more of their horses than of town, state, or national officials.

Accordingly, it seems foolish to dismiss minigovernments as possible subjects of rights, or to exclude employees from discussions of civil liberties. We have assumed that rights are not as important for employees as for political citizens. Our assumption is in error.

SUNRISE IN THE SALT MINES

Until the 1950s, employee constitutionalism was hypothetical. One could have traveled from Albuquerque (N.M.) to Zilwaukee (Mich.) without seeing a trace of it. In the 1960s, without forewarning, it appeared here and there in tenuous form. But no one took it seriously. Almost no one wrote about it.

And then, early in the 1970s, employee rights abruptly began to materialize. To most managers, employees, lawyers, journalists, and other people the movement still was unreal. To most of them it must have appeared outside the window like an apparition, a flying saucer. It still does. How are they to describe it? It conflicts with the accepted realities of past experience. As Gertrude Stein said, "There is no *there* there."

Yet there is.

In 1974 the highest state court in Pennsylvania came within a judicial whisker of standing a 3,000-year-old tradition on its head. By a vote of only 4 to 3 it upheld the venerable management prerogatives in a fairly clear-cut case of a corporate executive's "disobedience" of his superiors' desire to have him shut up. In another sector of the establishment the law had already been turned upside down. Beginning in 1968, the federal courts began to grant limited rights of speech to employees in certain types of public organizations. In later chapters these cases will be described in detail.

In the 1960s and especially in the early 1970s, a few leading corporations began experimenting with different approaches to employee constitutionalism. They did this with little fanfare. Apparently they felt no compulsion to innovate because of court decisions, labor unions, or government agencies. They did not act in concert. Indeed, an astonishing characteristic of this movement is the almost complete lack of communication between its various parts. The innovations just began appearing here and there, growing as silently as mushrooms. Several of these pioneering corporate efforts will be described in later chapters.

During the same period, several leading lawmakers seemed to hear the same drummer that the judges and business leaders heard. The solons began holding hearings and talking about laws to create employee rights. (These efforts, too, will be examined later on.)

In still another part of the establishment, such professional groups as the American Chemical Society and the American Association for the Advancement of Science began talking about rights like privacy and due process. In tactful ways these groups also began prodding employers to recognize such rights.

A few academics began using terms like "constitutionalism" and "due process" in scholarly papers. If the judges, solons, and business innovators read them, they made no mention of it. However, other teachers and researchers did, along with some students.

Ralph Nader and various of his associates gave sharp, hard support to employee rights at an early stage. They did not tread softly or delicately. They made noise, pushed, cajoled. Like a first wave assaulting a fortress, they were repulsed, but not before the traditionalists took note of them. When James M. Roche, chairman of General Motors, rhetorically shot down Ralph Nader in 1971, only the press paid much attention. In retrospect, however, Roche's broadside appears like a tribute, a kind of de facto recognition by conservative business leaders. It was proof that the concept of employee constitutionalism had in fact been seen, heard, and felt by reliable observers. Incensed by Ralph Nader's exhortations to employees to "rat" on management when they felt it was acting irresponsibly, Roche declared:

> Some of the enemies of business now encourage an employee to be disloyal to the enterprise. They want to create suspicion and disharmony, and pry into the proprietary interests of the business. However this is labelled—industrial espionage, whistle blowing, or professional responsibility—it is another tactic for spreading disunity and creating conflict.[11]

To the surprise of many, not all managers in business and government subscribed fully to this riposte. "Suppose top management is Watergating," managers wondered. "Is total obedience required then?" Replying to a lengthy questionnaire, more than 3,500 subscribers to the *Harvard Business Review* made it clear that a questioning of management's traditional prerogatives was going on in the executive ranks, too.[12]

And what about blue-collar and white-collar employees during the late 1960s and early 1970s? Perhaps their attitudes and actions were the surest sign of all that the seeds of constitutionalism, blown in perhaps from the political and social sectors, had at last taken hold in organizations. An Eastern Air Lines pilot refused to follow a fuel-jettisoning regulation which would have polluted the air; he was fired but the Airline Pilots Association and journalists came to his rescue, and later he was reinstated. A steel company worker refused to follow an order directing him to dump toxic materials into the Cuyahoga River; he was suspended but the union went to work and got the penalty revoked. An auto plant inspector in Michigan, incensed by some defective welding that the management was tolerating, turned information over to Ralph Nader. The inspector's bosses were furious but could not fire him because the union and Nader were ready to fight.

A changing attitude toward authority has impregnated the front lines—"the troops"—as well as jurists, legislators, managers, and others. In an unpublished position paper, U.S. Senator Charles Percy of Illinois referred to the "deep anger" he found among young workers at Lordstown, Ohio, scene of a bitter strike against General Motors in 1972. Percy said that one worker told a reporter: "Every time I passed through those plant gates to go to work, I left America, and my rights as a free man. I spent nine hours in there, in prison, and then came out into my country again."

In his talks with thousands of Illinois workers during the 1972 election campaign, Percy sensed more frustration than anger: "I heard more workers talking about the quality of life at work than I ever recall hearing before. Whenever I suggested finding new ways to give them a greater voice in workplace decisions, I could sense a new interest and excitement."

In short, many Americans have come to desire a new balance of employee rights and management prerogatives. This desire appears to be spreading. Each type of change just described has become visible to more observers in more ways. "A new idea has begun to rule America," sums up Duncan E. Littlefair. "This is the idea that no group or authority has a special claim to understanding, power, or influence."[13] One of England's new employee directors puts it in an earthier way. "The way I see it," he says of a 1973 decision putting him and several other workers on the board of British Steel Corporation, "we are in there . . . to challenge the bland assumption that management is always right."[14] He might be speaking for numerous employees on this side of the Atlantic as well.

The Vietnam War, Watergate, and other events doubtless had something to do with precipitating the new attitude. However, it is difficult to attribute it to any one sequence of events or to the influence of particular powers. Instead, the change seems to be one of subtle coloration, ubiquitous, undramatic—more like the profound alteration of sea and sky that sailors call a "sea change" than like a line storm.

Another curious thing about the new mood is that its logic, its rationale, appears to have been with us for many generations. If the employee rights movement were based on the merits alone, surely it would have appeared a century ago when business and public organizations grew sizable, impersonal, and hierarchal. The timing of the movement, therefore, may be more a function of broad changes in social attitudes than of perceived need.

AUTOCRACY—RARE, MEDIUM, OR WELL DONE?

Although many corporations and public agencies could be despotic if they chose to be, they are not. No law compels the managements to provide a fair and equitable environment, but many do that anyway, for reasons of their own.

Is an employee rights movement really necessary, then? With society as a whole becoming more rights-conscious, and with enlightenment spreading, may not corporations and agencies develop constitutionalism by osmosis?

Nobody knows how much despotism pervades the workplace. No agency takes complaints (except in special cases like equal employment opportunity, occupational safety legislation, and collective bargaining). No computer keeps track. After all, if employees have no guarantees of civil liberties, on what basis can records be made? When blacks were chattels, no one kept tabs on violations of their dignity by slave owners; and when women and children were nearly rightless, no one filed reports on acts of physical abuse inflicted by husbands and fathers.

Nonetheless, observation suggests that numerous employers have little respect for free expression, conscience, privacy, and other civil rights of employees. In many organizations the dominant reality is "management by fear." For all practical purposes, employees are required to be as obedient to their superiors, regardless of ethical and legal considerations, as are workers in totalitarian countries. An employee who is victimized by a boss is free only to take a cue from Shakespeare and "trouble deaf Heaven with my bootless cries."

How do we know this? We get candid, firsthand commentaries on life in organizations from reporters, business case writers, and employees themselves. We get reports from ombudspeople, arbitrators, and other investigators. We have the testimony recorded in trials in state and federal courts (some to be described in later chapters).

In addition, corporate leaders themselves have offered their impressions from time to time. "We stress the advantages of the free enterprise system, we complain about the totalitarian state," stated Robert E. Wood of Sears, Roebuck, "but in our individual organizations we have created more or less of a totalitarian system in industry, particularly in large industry."

Such evidence leaves no doubt whatever that tyranny at work is an important fact of life. America is not God's experiment, as the saying goes, for employees. In politics, schoolrooms, and community life, many of the old pains of mankind have been removed in the United States. But in much of the workplace despotism flourishes. Without minimizing the great and solid gains achieved by the unions, equal employment opportunity officials, occupational safety officials, and enlightened managements, let there be no doubt that much goes on which violates the average American's sense of justice and fair play. The only question is whether such violations characterize 40 percent, 60 percent, or some other proportion of organization life.

This conclusion stands even if generous allowances are made for the exigencies of efficient work and production. No realist will argue that companies, government bureaus, and other public agencies should be run democratically. There must be discipline. There must be control. There must be scope for quick and arbitrary judgments by decision makers. Otherwise there can be no efficiency, there can be little employee satisfaction with a job well done, and the impact on the cost of goods and services would be staggering.

In addition, most observers will agree that management is justified in drawing the line on some outside activities and behavior not immediately related to job performance. It may be important for sales people to join certain clubs and dress in certain ways. It may be important for employees in two competing companies not to hobnob with each other on the golf course. There may be plans and negotiations in the offing that should not be mentioned outside the organization, even in the most casual ways. There may be internal disputes that are nobody's business but those immediately concerned. In some settings, an employee's "moonlighting" activities may affect the organization so much that management is justified in intervening.

One could go on with numerous qualifications of this sort. They have to do with controls that are "reasonable" for management to require, the criterion for reasonableness being what knowledgeable observers agree is necessary for the efficient functioning of an organization. Therefore, it is not necessarily bad that an employee is fired for shooting his mouth off. It is not necessarily unjust that an employee's locker is opened in his or her absence. Much depends on the situation. In drawing the line in an organization, it is necessary to do the same thing we do in judging what is fair in community and political life; that is, try to put conflicting desires and interests in some sort of creative balance.

The prospects and consequences of employee constitutionalism depend on how we understand a series of issues that are open to debate:

1. *Can important new employee rights be justified legally and socially?* Working conditions in industry, government, education, and other fields are good in the United States. The common law, which is the foundation of employer prerogatives, has been built on centuries of experience. Moreover, there has been a long-term tendency to-

ward improvement. Therefore, would we do better to leave well enough alone?

2. *Can employee rights be justified economically—are they too costly?* Productivity in the business sector is high; in public organizations it may not be so high, but it still compares favorably with that in the rest of the world. Conceivably, constitutionalism could endanger the efficiency of organizations. To be realistic, what can we learn from the experience of organizations that have recognized one form or another of employee rights?

3. *If new rights are justified, what rights?* We might settle just for a few more rights in specific areas, such as protection for the employee who reports a violation in safety standards, as provided under Occupational Safety and Health Administration legislation. Or we might simply establish minimum rights for certain types of employees—for example, outlawing industry-wide "blacklisting" of a chemist or engineer who has resigned or been fired. At the other extreme, we might seek to establish the right to criticize publicly any and all decisions made by management; we might support an elaborate and formal process of review for all grievances; we might urge sweeping guarantees of privacy on the premises; and so on.

These are the possibilities. What should we try to achieve?

4. *How are employee rights to be enforced?* The whole concern with rights is meaningless if there are no realistic, practical ways of enforcing them. Some observers feel that the movement might founder on this question, for there are numerous subtle ways that an employer can retaliate against a dissident employee—ways that are most difficult to anticipate in legislation or prove in court with "hard" evidence.

Some possible methods of enforcement have already been used in a few organizations. Would they work on a larger scale? Other possibilities are judge-inspired changes in the common law, with courts providing remedies for penalized employees. Still other possibilities are anticipated in legislation already proposed. Might some of these approaches have practical value?

These and other questions will be pursued in the rest of this book. Although the questions cannot be separated neatly and disposed of individually, in general I will concentrate on the first two questions in Part II, the third question in Part III, and the fourth in Part IV.

NOTES

1. Mack Hanan, "Make Way for the Organization Man," *Harvard Business Review*, July-August 1971, pp. 135–136.
2. See Lawrence E. Blades, "Employment at Will vs. Individual Freedom: On Limiting the Abusive Exercise of Employer Power," *Columbia Law Review* 67 (1967):1405.
3. See David W. Ewing, "Employee Rights: Taking the Gag Off," *Civil Liberties Review*, Fall 1974, p. 56.
4. Timothy H. Ingram, "The Corporate Underground," *Nation*, September 13, 1971, p. 208.
5. 8 Pa. Comm. Ct. Reports 649,304 A. 2nd 380 (1973). Also see *New York Times*, August 26, 1973.
6. From Bob Cromie, "The Watergate Mother Goose," *Chicago Tribune*, November 4, 1973.
7. Blades, 1412.
8. See 299 F. Supp. 1100, cited in *Employee Relations in Action*, August 1971 (New York, N.Y., Man & Manager), pp. 1–2.
9. See, for example, Bernard Schwartz, *The Bill of Rights: A Documentary History*. Vol. 1 (Toronto and New York: Chelsea House Publishers in association with McGraw-Hill Book Company, 1971), pp. 435 ff.
10. Arthur Bentley, *The Process of Government*, cited in Arthur Selwyn Miller, *The Modern Corporate State* (Westport, Conn.: Greenwood Press, 1976), p. 188.
11. *New York Times*, March 26, 1971.
12. See David W. Ewing, "Who Wants Corporate Democracy?" *Harvard Business Review*, September-October 1971, p. 12, and "Who Wants Employee Rights?" *Harvard Business Review*, November-December 1971, p. 22.
13. Duncan E. Littlefair, *The Glory Within You* (Philadelphia: Westminster Press, 1973), p. 15.
14. Nancy Foy, "Workers on the Board—the Voices of Experience," in *Company Boards Tomorrow* (London: The Institute of Management Consultants and The Management Consultants Association, 1976), p. 33.

PART II

A Rationale
for Employee Rights

All animals are equal, but some animals are
more equal than others.

—George Orwell

2

THE
OUTMODED LAW
OF
EMPLOYER CHAUVINISM

When informed that the law considered a wife to be her husband's servant, in Dickens's *Oliver Twist,* Mr. Bumble retorted, "If the law supposes that, the law is a ass—a idiot." Though Bumble's famous opinion was accurate, it was not until recently, about a century later, that the domestic relations laws with their chauvinist assumptions began to be changed. For the traditional law had been in effect so long, and so many generations had grown up under it and got used to it, that an enormous effort was required to overcome the inertia of legislators and the vested interests of all those people and institutions who profited from the status quo.

Is the law of employee rights similarly out of date? Although it is not as ancient as the law of husband-wife relations, it is based on ideas thousands of years old. If those ideas are anachronisms, no law depending on them can be sound.

First of all, what precisely does the law say about employer and employee, boss and subordinate? Of particular importance, by what authority does an employer and his or her managers forbid to employees such rights as free speech and press, privacy, and refusal to obey an unethical or illegal directive?

Broadly speaking, the common law says that an employee

is an agent who is bound to be obedient and loyal to his or her principal, that is, to the employer or boss who, acting within the authorities given him by the employer, directs the employee at work. Sections 383 and 385 of the *Restatement of Agency* (as revised in 1958), which is the most authoritative summary of the law in this field, state that an agent has a duty to obey all "reasonable" directions of the principal. Comment *a* on section 385(1) states that the agent is not required to perform "illegal or unethical" acts, but as Dean Phillip I. Blumberg of the University of Connecticut Law School emphasizes, this only authorizes the employee to withdraw from the firm or public agency, not to deviate from the orders given or to disclose information about the organization against the employer's wishes.[1] Section 385(2) of the *Restatement* gives the agent an "out" in order to protect his or her economic interests, but the official commentary makes it clear that the public interest does not justify noncompliance with a boss's order.

Adding reinforcement to the concept of obedience, Section 387 states that an agent must be loyal to the employer or boss, acting solely for their benefit in all matters connected with the working relationship. Comment *b* on this section states that "the agent is also under a duty not to act or speak disloyally" except in the pursuit of his own interests outside work in the organization.

To leave absolutely no doubt that employers and senior managers can demand complete loyalty from subordinates and get it, the common law says the employer may discharge his employee at any time for any reason, so long as there is no statute or agreement limiting such right or discharge. *A fortiori*, the employer can transfer, promote, demote, or otherwise change an employee's status at any time. It does not matter if the boss is arbitrary or even wrong in taking such action. He doesn't have to give a good reason or any reason. For an employee to have a paycheck *and* rights of speech, conscience, and privacy, says the common law, is tantamount to running with the hare and hunting with the hounds.

An illustration of the immensity of the employer prerogative comes to me from a public health official in Ohio. After being made health commissioner in a certain city, not long ago, he displeased the municipal board of health by sending out a questionnaire to department heads asking them about the behavior of his predecessor in the health job. (The predecessor had acted erratically, in the opinion of various observers, and the new official sought evidence of this for a thesis he was writing for a master's degree in public administration at a well-known university.)

The board of health fired the new official summarily. He filed a suit in the appropriate federal court to force the board to reinstate him. In defense of its action, and worried about its civil rights posture, the board offered five work-related reasons, none of which had to do with the questionnaire. The judge found these reasons specious and ordered the board not to fire the official.

About three weeks after he resumed the job, the board of health fired him again, without a warning or hearing. The official went back to court to get reinstated, but this time the board was more clever: It gave *no* reason for the dismissal. This time the judge upheld the board—it was acting within its rights!

Looking back on the case, the official noted that the reasons for the second firing were clearly the same as the reasons for the first firing. When spelled out, they had infringed, in the judge's opinion, on the official's rights under the First Amendment. The official realized what an impossible box the law put him in during the second case. "How do you determine," he lamented, "if it was a constitutionally protected right if *no reason* is permitted to be given?"

In his treatise on employee rights,[2] Dean Lawrence E. Blades of the College of Law, University of Iowa, quotes from a number of decisions and authorities to show how firmly the courts have held to the traditional line. Here are a few statements of the law:

—Employers "may dismiss their employees at will . . . for good cause, for no cause, or even for cause morally wrong, without thereby being guilty of legal wrong." *Payne* v. *Western & A.R.R.*, 81 Tenn. 507, 519–520 (1884). The decision was overruled on appeal but on other grounds.

—The "arbitrary right of the employer to employ or discharge labor, with or without regard to actuating motives," is a proposition "settled beyond peradventure." *Union Labor Hospital Association* v. *Vance Redwood Lumber Co.*, 158 Cal. 551, 555 (1910).

—The relation of master and servant . . . casts certain duties upon . . . the servant, which he was bound to fulfill and discharge; and the principal one was that of obedience to all reasonable orders of . . . the master, not inconsistent with the contract. Disobedience of reasonable orders is a violation of the law which justifies . . . the peremptory discharge of the servant." *Mair* v. *Southern Minnesota Broadcasting Co.*, 226 Minn. 137, 138 (1948).

It is true that the business employer's once-absolute freedom to discharge has been restricted somewhat by state and federal statues and by collective bargaining agreements. However, the prerogative is still basically intact. For instance, in the famous *NLRB* v. *Jones & Laughlin Steel Corp.* case, where the Supreme Court upheld the National Labor Relations Act's protection of employees' right to unionize, the judges made it clear that the Act did not interfere with the "normal" exercise of the employer's right to discharge, but only with discharge when used to intimidate and coerce employees considering whether to unionize.[3] In a late 1975 case involving General Motors, the Supreme Court once again confirmed the traditional rule.[4]

In federal government agencies and companies manufacturing for the federal government, as we shall see in a later chapter, employer prerogatives have been curtailed further by the courts. Even here, however, the law has quite a way to go before "constitutionalism" becomes an appropriate description of the form of governance.

In sum, federal and state courts have been very conservative on the question of employer prerogatives. Even in the heralded decision on the *Zinman* case (see Chapter 1), the

Pennsylvania court did not question the need for the secretary to leave when she was unwilling to carry out the illegal and unethical order; it only decided she was eligible for unemployment compensation on the grounds she had compelling reasons to make an exit.

The basis for the courts' conservatism is the principle of freedom of contract, one of the best-guarded notions in Anglo-Saxon law. Employer and emplyee join hands willingly, the law says. They are equal partners to the employment agreement. Just as the employee is free to resign whenever he or she wants, so the employer is free to show him or her the door whenever it desires. In engineering terms, the courts see the employment bargain as a kind of "closed" system. That is, the bargain takes place independently of other forces and obligations in society (though of course it can be affected by other *contracts* employer or employee make).

How did the law get to be this way? Apparently it has never been otherwise, at least, not in most societies we know of. Lawrence Stessin, Professor Emeritus at Hofstra University, who publishes the newsletters of *Man and Manager,* believes the basic principle dates back to the Code of Hammurabi, in 632 B.C., which stated that an organizer could staff his workforce with the people he considered suitable. We know, too, that the rights of master and servant in ancient Roman law have been a model of the employment relationship in Anglo-Saxon law. For example, in the *Payne* v. *Western & A.R.R.* decision referred to by Dean Blades, the court wrote:

> May I not refuse to trade with any one? May I not forbid my family to trade with any one? May I not dismiss my domestic servant for dealing, or even visiting, when I forbid? And if my domestic, why not my farm-hand, or my mechanic, or teamster?[5]

Dean Blades also notes that the favored status of the employer in the common law appears to date back to the Black Death in England in the fourteenth century. With England's labor force reduced by almost one-half, and employers begging for workers, it made sense to stress employer prerogatives, and this was indeed done by the Ordinance and Statute of Labourers in the reign of King Edward III.[6] Thus, many employers have successfully sued individuals and organizations that have used unconventional means to lure or pirate away key employees.

When we recall that through most of human history, servants have been regarded as property, as chattels of the master, it is no wonder that legal thought has favored the employer rather than the employee. Not much more than a century ago, slaves were the legal property of their Southern owners in this country. Less than two centuries ago, in parts of Europe, vassals could be treated like perishable merchandise. Around 1789, historian Joseph Barry reports, the seigneur of the manor in various Western European cantons was authorized to have two of his vassals disemboweled on his return from the hunt so that he could "refresh his feet in their warm bodies."[7] Some vassals could be required to suckle the master's dogs.

Though such customs appear grotesque today, the belief that legitimated them still is held in esteem. This is the belief that the person of property, rank, and high station knows more about what is right than do less powerful people. "Godliness is in league with riches; it is only to the moral man that wealth comes," said Bishop Lawrence, the preacher of the church J. P. Morgan attended. Mogul Harry P. Cohn is reported to have upbraided his writers by saying, "I've got $25,000,000. Have *you* got $25,000,000? And that gives me the right to tell you what pictures are all about . . . ." When remarks like these are printed today, they produce a smile—but more because of their form than content. Stated less baldly, they confirm the beliefs of a substantial percentage of leaders in business and public life.

Every "Watergate" in organizational life, whether it be in the White House, the Central Intelligence Agency, or a corporation, is rationalized by its architects on the grounds that they "know better" than other people what can be justified in the public interest. The masterminds see themselves as possessing, because of their experience and position, not only a better grasp of operations, planning, and management, but also a surer understanding of morality and ethics. The earth revolves around them, and, in the words of Viscount Morley, "Where it is a duty to worship the sun, it is pretty sure to be a crime to examine the laws of heat."

Centuries-old notions about the master-servant relationship were not alone in nurturing the present law of employee rights. Classical capitalist economics, though a Johnny-come-lately compared with the thinking just described, also helped the law to develop as it did. Adam Smith's ideal of free, open, and multitudinous competition came to mean that, just as consumers should be free to choose from merchandise offerings, so workers should be free to go from one firm to another to take advantage of discrepancies in wage rates and working conditions. Great classical economists like Alfred Marshall, John Stuart Mill, and David Ricardo made high worker mobility a tenet of an efficiently functioning capitalist system. Whether the realities of worker mobility ever squared with the economic vision is a moot question, but in any case the law assumed that normally an employee—at least, an employee with marketable skills and desirable work attitudes—could leave one firm, if he wanted to, and find a comparable position in another organization. This assumption legitimated the legal notion of freedom of contract, mentioned earlier.

Perhaps the most important source of support of employer prerogatives was the attitude of *employees*. Poorly educated, poorly trained, and poorly motivated, as a rule, they were content to let wisdom and insight reside in the heads of organizations. Indeed, as Duncan E. Littlefair has pointed out, they lived vicariously through their government, military, church, and economic leaders, identifying them as "heroes."[8] Without this attitude, the "divine rights" of organization heads could not have persisted.

In this age of union militance and employee activism, it is easy to forget that only a half century or so ago it was not thought unusual or bizarre for workers at Ford Motor Company to give their all to accomplish management's "impossible dream" of 10,000-cars-a-day output:

> Men actually worked until they dropped in front of their machines trying to contribute to it. This was on both the Model A and the Model T. . . . There was actually a feeling of exultation when a certain goal was reached on time. . . . Men would go over to the superintendent's office and look at the chart showing the production of the day before, and you would see them at quitting time looking at it. Every time ten more motors were added, they would come back and some of them would say, "Come on, boys, tomorrow we will do better."[9]

Nor was it thought corny or quaint, as it would be today, that employees of some corporations sang company songs that exulted the organization as if it were a Big Ten football team. Here are a few lines from "Ever Onward," a song that IBM employees could be heard singing at get-togethers a few decades ago:

> Ever onward—ever onward!
> We're bound for the top never to fall!
> Right here and now we thankfully
> Pledge sincerest loyalty
> To the corporation that's the best for all!
> Our leaders we revere, and while we're here
> Let's show the world just what we think of them!
> So let us sing, men . . . .

PROPS THAT NO LONGER PROP

Today, as we are reminded continually by the news media, many once-prevalent attitudes toward authority have disappeared. One by one, the props that supported employer prerogatives have fallen away. While it is lawful still for employers to dictate employee silence on any or all matters outside the coverage of labor law, and to decide how much, if any, constitutionalism should be allowed, there is little logic for such one-sided power. The main reason for the present imbalance seems to be inertia, the glacierlike weight of the past. Let us look at some of the most important changes in the employer-employee relationship.

1. *"Freedom of contract" has become an anachronism.* Any validity this influential notion might once have had went up with the smoke of the industrial revolution. A great many, and possibly most, employees in business, government, education, and other organizations today find it more difficult and costly to find a new employer than an employer finds it to procure a new employee for a job opening. Thus, most of the freedom in freedom of contract belongs to the employer.

Is it really true that a talented and hard-working accountant, salesperson, or computer programmer, let us say, can clean out his or her desk at Company X, when it gives him the pink slip, and count on moving soon to a comparable job across town in Company Y? Of course not. The employee may be too specialized—he may be schooled in a product or paperwork specialty that no other company in town uses. Or, the company may be the only one of its kind in the town, with the nearest competitor that offers similar jobs being miles and miles away. Or, the employee may be considered too old, so that other companies hesitate to take him on, desiring more youthful recruits instead. Or, the employee may be strongly attached to the particular locality he lives in—pulling the children out of school and selling the house may be very upsetting.

For these or other reasons, numerous employees fear dismissal and go to great lengths to appear loyal to their bosses. "Larry Ross," an interviewee in Studs Terkel's book *Working,* says that loyalty is "the most stupid phrase anybody can use in business." The mobile employee, observes Ross, who is said to be an experienced observer, doesn't have to be loyal because he can probably gain something by moving out. But many workers aren't in this enviable position. "The only loyal people are the people who can't get a job anyplace else."[10]

Despite industrial and governmental restraining programs, many employees are apprehensive about being trained for a job in another organization. Other employees fear the loss of retirement income that would be theirs if they continued with their present employers. Despite our variegated culture, still others fear the change in life style or income level that might be necessitated by a job change.

In state and local governments, employee fears and feelings of dependence are compounded by what some regard as a scandalous feature of most pension programs. This is the provision that an employee forfeits a large proportion of his benefits if he leaves the government service before reaching retirement age.

Consequently, all these employees lack what the economist calls bargaining power. Feeling (rightly or wrongly) they are expendable, they become easy prey to a boss's demands. Here and there is a person with such exceptional skills or connections—or possibly an employment contract—that his leaving the organization could cause hardship to management, but instances of this sort are far from common.

2. *The psychology of dismissal puts the employee at a disadvantage.* The bargaining inequalities just described are aggravated by other connotations of dismissal from a good job. One sociologist calls dismissal "a kind of organizational equivalent of capital punishment."[11] In generations past, such a description might have been called nonsense, but it rings true to the experience of many people today. Losing a job has started some people on the road to alcoholism, broken-up marriages, and caused severe depression. The veteran observer whom Terkel calls Larry Ross describes the emotional "before and after" as follows:

A guy in a key position, everybody wants to talk to him. All his subordinates are trying to get an audience with him to build up their own positions. Customers are calling him, everybody is calling him. Now [following dismissal] his phone's dead. He's sitting at home and nobody calls him. He goes out and starts visiting friends, who are busy with their own business, who haven't got time for him. Suddenly he's a failure. Regardless what the reason was—regardless of the press release that said he resigned—he was fired.

The only time the guy isn't considered a failure is when he resigns and announces his new job. . . .[12]

This psychological reality did not exist when the law of employer prerogatives developed. To be sure, servants were dependent on their masters. However, in economies where neither specialization nor dependency had been developed to the point they are today, employment was not the key to one's life style. Only if we renounce industrialization and turn en masse to communes would the venerable rules about discharge make sense again.

3. *The "politics" of dismissal may be far more costly to the employee than to the employer.*

Underlying the thinking of economists and lawyers has been the assumption that an employer who unfairly or unwisely fires employees is penalized as much as they are. Not so. It is true that the employer may pay some price, especially if the discharged employees are professionals. For example, the American Chemical Association, in its publication *Chemical and Engineering News*, prints notices about companies that have treated its members with a heavy hand, and this publicity is considered to act as a restraint on employer prerogatives. (This subject will be considered in more detail in Chapter 11.) But as a general rule the discharged employee is likely to run into more obstacles than the organization does. This fact, too, destroys the equity of the traditional law of employer prerogatives.

In the first place, an employee who bucks management and loses can and often does run afoul in the network of supplier, customer, and other business connections that surrounds an organization. Let me give one example:

After six years as a well surveyor with Company A, a geologist was suddenly dismissed because of a personality clash with his boss. Only one other firm in the region did the same kind of work that Company A did, so the geologist applied to that firm and, after a five-month wait, was hired. To his dismay, however, he found himself reporting to his old boss again; during the interim period, the boss had also transferred to the new firm. Not surprisingly, the geologist found himself on the street once more after a few months of tension with the boss.

The geologist then attempted to start his own business in the well-surveying field. When he tried to purchase the necessary equipment, however, he found that it could be procured only from Company A and the second firm. Each refused to sell him the machines and instruments he needed.[13]

This case may sound unusual but it is not. For example, in one common variation, the discharged employee finds that his or her new boss is a friend of the boss with whom he or she had the run-in. In all such variations, the employee suffers mightily while the organizations are only inconvenienced.

Second, the discharged employee may find himself or herself under a cloud because he is not a "team player." Especially if he leaves because of a disagreement over the morality, legality, or responsibility of the employer's actions, the word may spread ahead of him to other organizations that he is a "nice guy but a trouble maker." It is a gossamer web of hostility, made up of hearsay and "Oh, by the way"-type remarks during phone calls and coffee breaks at conventions, yet it can penalize the free speaker with devastating efficiency.

The moral is that, to avoid such penalization, an employee should not specify his reasons when he resigns over a moral issue. By definition, however, this path is not chosen by the whistle-blower and dissident—they have stood up already and been counted in opposition. Labeled as kooks, they are politely rejected by other employers.

In their book *Resignation in Protest,* Edward Weisband and Thomas M. Franck create an imaginary dialogue with George Ball, who resigned as Under-Secretary of State in 1966 because he disagreed with the Johnson Administration's support of the Vietnam War. Suppose Ball had asked them, the authors say, whether he should lead a public campaign against the war. How should they have replied? They should have told him that it would be a good idea from the standpoint of the republic. He would have enhanced public understanding and perhaps saved the country billions of dollars as well as many lives. On the other hand, they would have had to advise him that speaking out would have ended his political career and led to his being ostracized in professional circles. "You have spent your life as a team player, a loyal peer-grouper. You would suddenly have found yourself being categorized as a non–team player by that small elite on whose amiability your professional and private life is built. The costs to you would have been enormous."[14]

At least until the traditional law is brought in line with current realities, the same advice would have to be offered many an employee who is offended by wrongdoing in the organization.

Third, the discharged employee may be penalized by industry blackballing. Since employers do not have to contend at all with this risk, it operates exclusively in their favor and makes the notion of bargaining equality more preposterous still.

It is difficult to tell how much blackballing goes on in industry and government, partly because it is hard to prove. No doubt many fierce allegations of blackballing have been unfounded—they are all-too-convenient rationalizations for bitter employees who can't understand why their talents don't impress would-be employers. Yet many astute observers with whom I have talked believe that a great deal of blackballing goes on in educational, corporate, and governmental worlds.

More and more, thoughtful employers disdain blackballing, regarding it as neither ethical nor necessary. One day the practice itself will be "blackballed" in laws and codes. Because it is so difficult to police, however, it is likely to be a factor in employer-employee bargaining for some years to come.

4. *Corporations are no longer simply economic animals.*

Centuries ago, it made sense to apply the ancient principle of master and servant to employers and employees in commerce because companies were seen as the private enterprises of their owners. Does that view make sense today when corporations have come to wield an ever-more-direct influence on national security and welfare?

As Dean Blumberg has pointed out, the *Restatement of Agency*, with its careful proscriptions and prescriptions for agents (employees) and principals (employers or bosses), assumes an economic-only view of a business. Based on common-law cases, it is concerned almost solely with economic activity, economic advantage, economic motivation, economic loyalty. (Only when the boss is bent on legal wrongdoing does the *Restatement* let the junior employee off the hook for disloyalty to him.) Hence the rules given in the *Restatement* are irrelevant to the employee rights movement, which stresses an employee's role as a social and moral citizen along with his role as worker. "The question may fairly be asked," Blumberg notes, "to what extent the *Restatement* and the common-law decisions are useful in the analysis of a proposal that rests on the concept of an agent's primary obligation as a citizen to the society, transcending his economic duty to the principal."[15]

In later chapters we shall examine more fully the changing nature of the corporation.

5. *Employees are willing to question the moral, legal, and philosophical judgments of their superiors.*

Employees accept that management must manage, that the boss has to make planning and operating decisions. This understanding comes as naturally as that a football or baseball team can't operate democratically. What many people in business and government are challenging is the idea that top management possesses superior wisdom on questions of moral, ethical, and legal behavior. This was the great lesson of the public revolts over the Vietnam War and the Watergate affair: even the U.S. president has no superior claim to an understanding of "rightness," no matter how confidential and complicated the operations in question.

The law of master and servant, the traditional rules authorizing an employer to discharge an employee for any reason or no reason at all, are inconsistent with this newer *Zeitgeist*. Like male chauvinism, employer chauvinism has become an inappropriate basis for human relations and governance.

With more and more Americans becoming dependent on sizable organizations for employment, and with more organizations exercising greater power over the individual in their role as suppliers of products, energy, entertainment, education, regulation, and other services, it will be surprising if the courts do not carve up the outmoded common law rules. Indeed, as we shall see in later chapters, they have already cut them back a little here and a little there. The time may not be far off when a court opinion echoes the following conclusion of Dean Blades:

> The judiciary has not been reluctant to expand the meaning of constitutional provisions in order to protect the individual from governmental oppression. It is something of a paradox that the courts have so far displayed no similar bent for invention and improvisation when it comes to protecting individuals, particularly in their highly vulnerable status as employees, from the private establishments upon which they are becoming increasingly dependent. Instead, there has been a blind acceptance of the employer's absolute right of discharge.[16]

NOTES

1. Phillip I. Blumberg, "Corporate Responsibility and the Employee's Duty of Loyalty and Obedience: a Preliminary Inquiry," *Oklahoma Law Review*, August 1971, p. 284.
2. Lawrence E. Blades, "Employment at Will vs. Individual Freedom: On Limiting the Abusive Exercise of Employer Power," *Columbia Law Review* 67 (1967): 1404; see 1405, 1406, and 1416.
3. *NLRB* v. *Jones & Laughlin Steel Corp.*, 301 U.S. 45–46 (1937). Cited in Blades, 1418.
4. *Percival* v. *General Motors Corporation*, 400 F. Supp. 1322 (1975).
5. *Payne* v. *Western & A.R.R.*, 81 Tenn. 507, 519–520 (1884). Cited in Blades, 1416.
6. Blades, 1416.
7. Joseph Barry, *Passions and Politics* (New York: Doubleday & Company, Inc., 1972), p. 364.
8. Duncan E. Littlefair, *The Glory Within You* (Philadelphia: Westminster Press, 1973), pp. 16–18.
9. Allan Nevins and Frank Ernest Hill, *Ford: Expansion and Challenge, 1915–1933* (New York: Charles Scribner's Sons, 1957), pp. 525–526.
10. Studs Terkel, *Working* (New York: Pantheon, 1974) p. 409.
11. Wilbur E. Moore, *The Conduct of the Corporation* (New York: Random House, 1962), p. 28.
12. Terkel, p. 410.
13. *Hinds* v. *Variton and Ledrane*, 390 F. Supp. 685 (1975); reported in *White Collar Management* (799 Broadway, New York, N.Y. 10003), November 1975.
14. Edward Weisband and Thomas M. Franck, *Resignation in Protest* (New York: Grossman, 1975), p. 191.
15. Blumberg, pp. 288–289.
16. Blades, 1435.

3

"WE SOUGHT WORKERS, AND HUMAN BEINGS CAME INSTEAD"

The notion that plants, offices, and agencies are populated by "economic man" apparently became popular in the West during the nineteenth century, a period when most business and public leaders were extremely conscious of their Christianity. Yet it is one of the most irreligious notions ever conceived. It was encouraged by the doctrines of "scientific management." Yet it violates the first principle (empirical observation) of the scientific method. It was nurtured with the motive of increasing productivity and solidifying management's position. Yet, though it succeeded at first in accomplishing those ends, it has done as much as any other philosophy, and more than communism or socialism, to produce industrial unrest and stimulate organized opposition to management power.

An employee is not divided, like Gaul, into three parts: breadwinner, private citizen, and soul. By virtue of his humanity, his economic, social, and religious natures are not and cannot be compartmentalized. They infuse one another. In fact, there is no such thing as a human "worker," there are only people who spend parts of their lives in workplaces. Though it is convenient to use the term "worker" in communication to denote a part-time activity, in reality the only true workers are inhuman. They are the robots, such as those manufactured by Unimation and AMF, that do spot welding, unloading, lifting and placing, picking, and other repetitive-motion tasks.

Wherever the illusion of "economic man" persists, it is difficult to justify employee rights. The only arguments that hold water are those showing that productivity may increase, unions may be kept out, political power may be gained, and so forth. Such results may indeed happen, if employee rights are established, but they are not the real justification. Since the whole notion of "economic man" is false, its framework cannot accommodate the most important reason that employee rights are valid and desirable. This reason is that people function best *as* people, and in the long run they will settle for no system that limits them to "economic" functions.

By the same token, where a realistic, empirical, scientific view of employees is held, the case for employee rights is obvious and simple. How else can an employee be treated as a dignified human? There may be real difficulties in implementing rights, for generally they are seen as a threat by at least some managers, but these practical problems can be solved, given sufficient time.

When a country is excited by the first advances into material prosperity, as the United States was in the nineteenth century and other societies have been more recently, it is easier to be deluded by the notion that a person at work sheds his individuality and thinks only about paychecks, seniority, productivity, coffee breaks, safety, working hours, and so forth. When a person is hungry enough, he or she doesn't resent being treated, as Balthazar put it in Lawrence Durrell's *Justine*, as "just a passage for liquids and solids, a pipe of flesh." Mohandas Gandhi phrased the thought more eloquently when he said that God cannot appear to the hungry except in the form of bread.

Moreover, when employees are caught in dull, dreary jobs and feel there is no way out, their behavior may confirm the "economic man" doctrine—for a while. They daydream in order to put up with the monotony. Some actually seek out the most repetitive tasks available to make mental escape easier. Rather than be morons, they act like morons so they can escape from the workplace.

But as a society (or a group within a society) becomes more affluent and more advanced, inevitably people take the necessities of living for granted and become concerned with more sophisticated values. Abraham Maslow said it all with his five-level hierarchy of needs. (See Figure 1.) The basic need is food, clothing, and shelter for survival (level 1), Maslow said; once this need is satisfied, man begins to think about safety and security (level 2); when this need is satisfied, needs for belonging, sharing, and association (level 3) become important; then come the so-called ego needs of achieving, developing self-confidence, winning recognition, and asserting one's independence (level 4); and the highest level, which becomes important after ego needs begin to be satisfied, is self-fulfillment, that is, the desire to express one's whole range of potential to be a thinking, loving, spiritual human being (level 5).

In the United States and other advanced nations, people can be found seeking satisfaction at each of these five levels. But whereas a century ago, perhaps the majority were at the first and second levels, and fifty years ago at the second and third levels, today the drift is definitely toward the third, fourth, and sometimes fifth levels.

It is hard to think of any trend that more surely discredits the "economic man" doctrine, leaving it an empty footnote for history. To seek Maslow's third- and fourth-level needs is to seek to relate oneself to the larger community of which the employer organization is but a part, and to apply to life in the organization the ethical, moral, and social principles which one finds satisfying as a thinking, inquiring citizen.

"We sought workers, and human beings came instead," Max Frisch once said. A perspicacious shoe manufacturer in Milwaukee, Henry Nunn, put the same thought in the title of his book, *The Whole Man Goes to Work*.[1] More recently, thoughtful observers have been making statements such as the following:

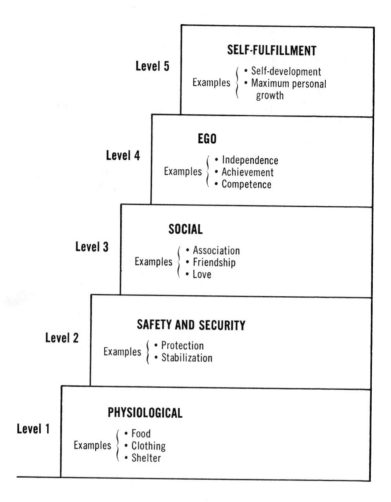

Fig. 1. Abraham Maslow's hierarchy of human needs.

A business corporation, like a university, or a government agency, or a large hospital—each with its hierarchy and status system—is now a lifetime experience for many of its members. Necessarily, therefore, it can no longer be an instrument satisfying a single end—in the case of the business corporation, only turning out its goods and services—but it has to be a satisfactory way of life for its members. It not only has to satisfy its customers; it has to be agreeable to its "self" —Daniel Bell, *The Coming of Post-Industrial Society*.[2]

The community is increasingly in the organization. It will be the job of management to make the individual's values and aspirations redound to organizational energy and performance. . . . Management will increasingly be concerned as much with the expression of basic beliefs and values as with the accomplishment of measurable results. It will increasingly stand for the quality of life of a society as much as for its standard of living—Peter Drucker, *Management*.[3]

Reaching out for higher-level satisfactions, growing more sensitive to the relationships between themselves, their employers, and the community, Americans wonder if it is enough to have rights only as political and social citizens. What about as employees, too? In our advanced, industrial society it seems unrealistic to hope that elected representatives, political ombudspeople, and labor unions can offer the guarantees necessary for the "whole man" to assert his individuality and self-esteem at work. These important agents can win some but by no means all of the rights that loom large at the third, fourth, and fifth levels of Maslow's hierarchy. The realization is growing that our actual freedom, as opposed to the conventionally interpreted constitutional freedom, is determined not alone by the power of political officials, judges, and policemen, but also, and perhaps more importantly, by the power of employers.

Sensitive business leaders do not need to be told which way the wind is blowing. The following observation comes from Dr. James G. Affleck, chief executive of American Cyanamid Company:

More and more, individuals are bringing to their jobs the interests and attitudes they have developed earlier, or which relate to their "private lives" outside the factory or office. It is becoming less and less possible to drop a curtain separating the corporate person from the private person, offering one set of incentives and rewards to each half while keeping them unrelated.[4]

To visualize what is happening, it may be useful to look at another scheme of aspirations, what I call the hierarchy of rights and privileges. As Figure 2 shows, it contains four levels:

Legal—the desire to be entitled to due process in courts of law and other tribunals, and to procedural and substantive rights in conflicts with the police and military authorities.

Political—the desire to exercise rights of expression, choice, privacy, property, and limited control over and against the government, ruling political parties, and so forth.

Social—the desire of members of a community to have equal opportunity, status, and standing in civic groups and social organizations regardless of differences in ethnic origin, race, creed, or sex.

Organizational—the desire not only for equal opportunity to obtain jobs and promotion in organizations, but also to enjoy limited rights of free expression, conscience, due process, and ethical independence as an employee, regardless of job position, status, ownership power, or length of service.

For several centuries Americans have enjoyed rights at the legal level, and at the political level since 1783. Since the end of the nineteenth century they have been gaining important rights at the socio-economic level. Beginning more recently, with corporate experiments in participative work management, a sprinkling of court decisions on employee rights, and certain legislation with protection for the whistle-blower, employees have been winning rights at the organizational level.

In other words, the American pattern has been to build the pyramid of rights from the ground up. The tendency has been to establish one new level of rights before moving on

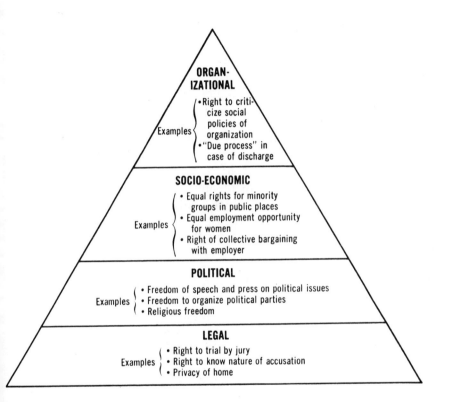

Fig. 2. Hierarchy of human rights.

to the next. Work at the lower levels continues, but each succeeding level is the foundation for its successor. Thus, organization rights have had to wait until today, for they could not be created successfully until much of the work had been done on socio-economic rights. In turn, socio-economic rights had to wait upon the establishment of substantial political rights, the level below them.

In some other countries the same general pattern appears to have been followed. In England, legal rights began developing in the reign of Alfred the Great; that country's magnificent system of common law has never stopped growing, and where its shoots took hold in the British colonies they have grown steadily, too, with the conspicuous exception of India. As for political rights, Magna Charta was the first step, and important later steps were taken in the eighteenth and nineteenth centuries. The rise of social rights was roughly coincidental with its rise in the United States. At the organizational level, unions have been winning rights since the 1930s, but in the development of speech and press rights, as well as participative work management, British employees seem to lag behind the Americans.

Scandinavia is notable for its leadership in organizational rights. Companies like Volvo, Kockums, and Granges, in Sweden, and Norsk Hydro, in Norway, have pioneered in creating employee rights of free speech, privacy, and due process. These companies had earlier pioneered in developing various forms of participative work management. Of course, the Scandinavian countries did not attempt organizational rights until they had a firm foundation of legal, political, and social rights.

In the Soviet Union rights have been slow to develop. As readers of Dostoevski know, Czarist Russia in the nineteenth century had courts for the protection of legal rights, and in recent years the court system has been expanding rapidly. However, even at the legal rights level in the Soviet Union there are enormous lacunae, with security and military forces enjoying immense advantages. Only the most primitive political rights are allowed by the Communist Party. Social rights have been established since Lenin took power after the Revolution. Organizational rights, not surprisingly, are probably more retarded in the Soviet Union than in any other industrialized nation.

One conspicuous exception to the rule that organizational rights do not materialize until after legal, political, and social rights develop is Yugoslavia. Under Marshal Tito's brand of communism, political rights were negligible. Yet in the 1960s Yugoslav enterprises began experimenting with extensive rights of worker self-management and also rights of expression. Workers have a powerful voice in decisions concerning hours, pay scales, prices, mergers, and even investment; the so-called workers' councils are the most important agency for wielding this power, but mass assemblies are held on occasion so employees can speak, argue, and vote on management questions.

Figure 3 shows some events and decisions that have shaped the growth of legal, political, social, and organizational rights in the United States. Note the differences in "starting times" among the classes of rights.

EVEN BENIGN BUREAUCRACIES DON'T SATISFY

Why is it that the magnificent efforts to make work more interesting and rewarding—job enrichment, job enlargement, organizational development, and the rest—have not satisfied employees' need for a voice in management? After all, the problems that concern an employee most are those in and around his own job—how work is arranged, scheduled, shared, quality-controlled, paid, and so forth. Is it just greed that prompts employees to want still more control and rights?

The trouble is that bureaucracy, even the most benign and enlightened bureaucracy such as that found in leading corporations, tends by its very nature to stultify. Therefore employees need all the compensating rights and privileges

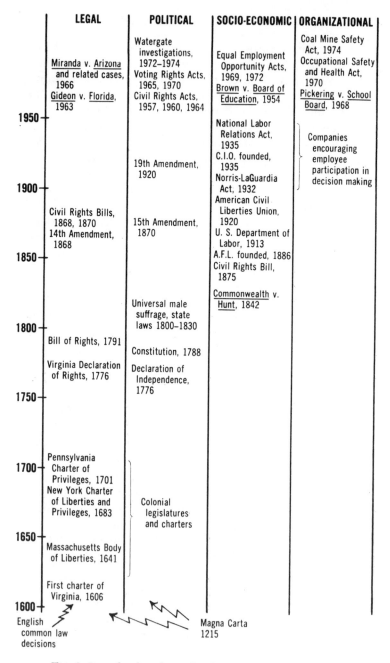

Fig. 3. Some landmarks in the development of U.S. rights.

they can exercise without jeopardizing management's right to manage. They need unions and associations, right-to-bargain laws, safety and work condition laws, fair wages and salaries, job enrichment, *and* rights of expression, due process, and ethical integrity. Without all of these compensations there is no possibility of the "whole man" going to work.

In a remarkable article published in a company magazine of Unilever, a factory manager declares:

> It is my submission that the worker in the large industrial enterprise is accorded the status of a child. In his domestic life he is invited, and indeed expected, to plan his affairs properly; to assume responsibility for the care of his dependents; and generally to pattern his behaviour along adult lines. When he walks into the factory he is given a number; "punches the clock"; is closely supervised; and is assumed to be capable of accepting no more than a bare minimum of responsibility. If he then reacts to this in either an apathetic or aggressive manner, management reacts by tarting up the physical environment or putting another quid in the wage packet, and is comfortably confirmed in its stereotype of the average worker as solely motivated by irrational and childish impulses. If, in desperation, the worker then latches on to the "militant" who appears to offer hope of escape from this morass, he is branded a sheep.[5]

This indictment is too harsh for thousands of companies in Europe and the United States, and especially for numerous employees who do not work on assembly lines. Prune back some of the abrasiveness, however, and it is applicable to employee groups in almost every sizable organization. For the objective of energetic management always is to control. If managers are to manage, they have to control—there is no alternative. Yet by definition, control means according employees the status of juniors. Although management may not control them as young children, as the Unilever manager assumes—it may consider them more like teen-agers—it still has to assume they are not as wise and far-seeing as itself. However unwritten or even unconscious the assumption, it comes through to employees. And so they are not as grateful and responsive as management wishes; restively they begin looking for more.

Why the seemingly unquenchable quest for more, always more? It is not the result of greed for power, or envy of management, or delusions of grandeur—employees are not like the archangel in Milton's *Paradise Lost*, who was not content to sit next to God but sought to become God. I suggest that the trouble may be simply discontent with self—lack of self-esteem caused by bureaucratic control. It is an old and cancerous problem, known in many ages and in most societies, from the United States to the Soviet Union. "The main misfortune, the root of all evil to come," said Boris Pasternak, "is the loss of confidence in the value of one's own opinion." How do organizations create such a feeling?

One of the most devastating analyses of bureaucracy comes from Erich Fromm:

> What would be a general definition of the bureaucratic method? There are many definitions and much has been written about bureaucracy. I remind all those who are interested in this especially of the work of Max Weber, which gave a great impetus to the study of bureaucracy in the United States. Let me suggest a very simple definition: *bureaucracy is a method of managing in which people are dealt with as if they were things. . . .*[6]

Fromm gives the example of the classroom. When a good instructor is teaching, he or she is relating to the student and in tune with him; he is sensitive, responsive, and "at one" with the student. There is no control—the teacher does not seek to control the student for his own self-aggrandizement. But when the student comes in to take an examination, the instructor becomes a policeman, administrator, and judge. Now his duty is not to give and respond to the student but to watch him suspiciously and evaluate. In this situation the instructor takes an authoritarian, bureaucratic role, and the student has become an object, a thing to be directed.

Necessarily, an executive acts in the same manner toward an employee, as does a judge to the defendant who is found guilty and now must be sentenced, and as does the nurse who treats a patient like a machine that is being fixed.

The technical expression for what happens when a manager watches a subordinate with a detached attitude, says Fromm, is *reification*. And when the employee becomes reified, he also becomes frightened (though he may not be aware of it) because he is not made to be treated impersonally by his fellow man.

Fromm goes on to say:

We can differentiate between two kinds of bureaucratic attitudes which I am sure you will all identify immediately. One is the *friendly bureaucrat*. His "friendliness," nevertheless, does not alter the fact that the other person is an "object" to him, just as he can be friendly to his car and to other things he uses. These friendly bureaucrats usually have a friendly disposition, or they fake it, because it is in the nature of their particular position and method of management that they have to appear to be friendly.

Quite different from the friendly, though indifferent bureaucrat is the *authoritarian-sadistic bureaucrat* who is somewhat more old-fashioned. I had an experience with one such individual the other day—I still travel by train, as my last-ditch battle against the American railroad companies. I went to Pennsylvania Station to buy a ticket to Mexico, and the man behind the ticket window told me that as of the end of that year the pullman service from St. Louis to Laredo would be discontinued, and he said, *"I'm glad about it.* I'm really glad about it." Then he added, "All that work, such a difficult ticket to make out!" (The difficult work is caused by not having a printed ticket, but having to write a ticket from here to St. Louis and from St. Louis to Mexico City.) This is the sadistic-authoritarian bureaucrat. Here was a man about 55 years of age; so he has been working for the railroads for 30 years. By discontinuing passenger travel his own job will be slowly abolished. He has grown up in this activity, and yet he is glad about its destruction. He is also so passive that even the small amount of activity involved in writing out a more difficult ticket than the usual one is to him only a disagreeable chore. . . .

The friendly bureaucrat is the more modern type of bureaucrat, the one who has learned how to "oil" people so that they work with less friction. The older type of bureaucrat, the authoritarian character, is more often to be found in conservative enterprises like railroads, shipping, post offices, law courts, etc.

But in spite of these differences between the "friendly" and the "authoritarian-sadistic" bureaucrat, they have one important quality in common: that they relate themselves to the other person as to a thing, as to an object—that they do not experience the other as a person and hence relate themselves to him without empathy or compassion.[7]

The evidence of Fromm's indictment is so common and widespread that it is part of our common knowledge. When an aide to former President Richard M. Nixon questioned the legality of some methods to be used in the Daniel Ellsberg case, the President replied: "I don't give a good Goddamn about that; it's more important to find the source of these leaks rather than worry about the civil rights of some bureaucrats." Ironically, Nixon himself was acting out the archetypal bureaucratic role—people are means to ends.

In his personal account of life at the upper levels of ITT, Thomas S. Burns recounts many examples of an identical attitude.[8] Large corporations are totalitarian, runs the message throughout this documentary, and in a totalitarian system a person's importance depends on his efficacy in accomplishing sales, profits, and other organizational objectives. You never disagree with the big boss—at least, not in such a manner that he thinks of it as disagreement.

The irony is that so often the leaders of business, government, and educational organizations don't want employee life to be this way. They idealize initiative, freedom of choice, imagination, bold thinking—all the qualities that are important to them as top executives. Again and again the chief executive exhorts managers and employees down the line to exercise these qualities. But bureaucracy and chain of command don't tolerate them easily. The reality is so obvious that it is painful to put in words: Though top executives, public relations people, and professors may not always believe it, and may, in fact, find the truth nearly incredible, institutions cannot be described by their charters, stated objectives, or wishes of top management. As Stafford Beer, president of the British Operations Research Society, observed soberly in a keynote address to that society in 1974, "Institutions are systems for being what they *are* and doing what they *do*."

It is no wonder, therefore, that employees may feel half-suffocated and long to cry out, the more so as the bureaucracy becomes more efficient and the supervisory control systems more advanced. The employee may even have the nightmarish feeling sometimes that management control systems lie close upon the workplace, and that (to paraphrase Lawrence Durrell) he works in between them, breathing through the eye of a needle.

NOTES

1. Henry Nunn, *The Whole Man Goes to Work* (New York: Harper & Row, 1953).
2. Daniel Bell, *The Coming of Post-Industrial Society* (New York: Basic Books, 1973), p. 288.
3. Peter Drucker, *Management* (New York: Harper & Row, 1974), p. 35.
4. James G. Affleck, *Management for the Future* (New York: McGraw-Hill Book Company, 1977).
5. Ian Cameron, "In Defense of Conflict?" *Unilever Magazine,* September-October 1974, p. 30.
6. Erich Fromm, "Thoughts on Bureaucracy," *Management Science,* August 1970, p. B-701.
7. Fromm, pp. B-703–704.
8. Thomas S. Burns, *Tales of ITT: An Insider's Report* (Boston: Houghton Mifflin Co., 1974).

4

ARE
EMPLOYEE RIGHTS
A THREAT
TO CAPITALISM?

Karl A. Menninger once observed that when a trout rising to a fly gets hooked on a line, he splashes and struggles to escape. Similarly, the great psychiatrist said, human beings struggle with the hooks that catch them in the environment. And just as it is hard for a free fish to understand what is happening to a hooked one, it is hard for people who are satisfied with the status quo to understand the efforts of those who are struggling with new problems and needs, such as employee rights and constitutionalism in organizations. The dissidents and activists appear to be acting irrationally—tearing the house down without rebuilding what they destroy. Their song may sound like "We don't know where we're going but we know we're on our way." However, for the struggling ones themselves there is no alternative, for they cannot accept the status quo.

What is happening to people's values? What changes in attitudes toward American institutions lie behind the words and actions of those who appear to threaten the rights of managers to manage and of owners to own?

One of the most important new beliefs is that the rights of private ownership, while important, must be qualified. In the United States, Britain, France, Germany, and many other countries, the well-accepted view during the eighteenth and nineteenth centuries was that an owner of land, factories, and capital could use or misuse, change or dispose of, preserve or exploit his property almost without restriction. Until the Great Depression and World War II there were few critics of the nearly absolute prerogatives of ownership.

Now that philosophy has withered in favor of ideals of social responsibility and accountability. The recognition that resources are limited and the environment fragile has accelerated the change, but it was on its way long before the Club of Rome and OPEC were dreamt of. Theologian Duncan E. Littlefair has expressed the new attitude toward ownership as follows:

> We must grow in awareness that the things that are ours in legal title are ours only temporarily. The raw materials of the land and the skills that design and manufacture the materials are, in effect, lent to us for a while. The land and its resources were here before we arrived, and the human skills are descended from generations that lived before we arrived. The process will continue after we die, with others being recipients of such loans while they live.[1]

In the view of Littlefair and others, legal title is a convenience—a very important and practical convenience yet something less than a holy verity.

Views like this make the corporation in particular vulnerable. Not too long ago private enterprise was virtually a "given" in Western societies. Now all of a sudden it must justify itself. A corporation is unlike an individual, who is important simply because he or she exists, says corporate attorney William T. Gossett. A corporation "is without inherent value . . . valuable only insofar as it serves people. It cannot, therefore, behave cavalierly, as some individuals can."[2]

For many decades corporate heads were free to feel that their organizations were like personal toys. "If you own it, it's yours to play with," the law said, in effect. But in 1877 Chief Justice Morrison R. Waite shot one hole in that concept when he wrote the famous *Munn* v. *Illinois* decision holding that property "affected with a public interest"—in particular, a privately owned company whose operations affect the community—cannot be regarded as the owners' private and personal affair. However, it was to take more than one Supreme Court decision to destroy the notion of corporate unaccountability. Not until after World War II had so many holes been shot in the concept that it began sinking out of sight.

If one incident stands for the final disappearance of the notion of corporate unaccountability, it might be an administrative decision affecting Howard Hughes. This brilliant but secretive entrepreneur presumed that because he owned Hughes Aircraft Company, he could do anything with it that he chose. According to Peter Drucker, the U.S. Air Force, which was the company's main customer, disagreed.[3] Either you put your shares in trust and let professional management take over, the Air Force said in the early 1950s, or we'll ground your firm, put it in bankruptcy, and force you out. Hughes acquiesced, relinquishing control but keeping ownership title through a foundation.

A decade or so later, Hughes was still acting out his belief with other companies he controlled. The management of TWA, of which Hughes was the main owner, sued him for $150 million, claiming he was subordinating the company's interest to that of other firms he owned. In a long court fight, winding up in the Supreme Court in 1973, the principle that an owner is not free to play with his company as he wishes was upheld. However, Hughes escaped having to pay damages because of a technicality.

The logic of corporate accountability is compelling. If we say, as we always have, that government agencies, universities, and "public" organizations in general cannot be operated as their leaders please because they affect the public interest, it follows that Union Carbide, American Motors, Shell Oil, Ralston Purina, and any number of other sizable companies cannot be operated selfishly either. Is the production and distribution of chemicals, transportation, energy, and food any less in the public interest than securities regulation, education, and public welfare?

"But we invested our hard-earned earnings in these companies," corporate leaders say. "These enterprises were only a dream we had, not so long ago. These organizations were not created by legislative vote and public funds. These organizations rose from our sweat and blood."

It is amazing how durable this belief has been. Despite being killed repeatedly by court decisions, legislative acts, and business schools, it keeps running in circles in the executive suite, like a chicken after its neck is broken. To proponents it never seems to occur to ask: How long would these companies last if society did not keep law and order? How long would they last if they could not recruit workers trained by public schools to read and write? If there were no churches and civic groups struggling with the community's ethical and moral questions?

Now consider how the new concept of corporate accountability affects the employee rights picture. So long as a company was the personal toy of its owner-managers, employees had a weak case for rights of speech, press, due process, privacy, and other matters. It was consistent for the boss to say, "If you don't want to play according to my rules, get out." But once society says a company has obligations to a wider constituency than owners, employees can develop a strong case.

After all, who has a bigger stake in an organization than those who invest all or part of their working lives in it? Without taking anything away from the vital roles of capital and top management, how long could the organization last without sales, production, secretarial, and other people? It seems safe to say that the president of, say, IBM would more quickly notice the absence of his executive secretary or Washington office manager than of an owner holding a hundred shares. (IBM has about 600,000 stockholders.)

Another ideological change affecting employee rights concerns the role of profit. In the gospel according to Locke,

Smith, Mill, and von Mises, it is easy to assemble evidence that the pursuit of profit is the DNA of GNP growth. Profit is the reward of individualism, the sugar plum that entices risk takers. If a company makes a profit, that fact alone justifies its existence, so long as it operates within the law. It is irrelevant whether employees want constitutionalism. "At Carthage, nothing which results in profit is regarded as disgraceful," stated Polybius in the *Histories*. For generations many missionary capitalists went farther than this: "In the United States, nothing which results in profit can be tampered with."

This philosophy has become as passé as Victor Herbert's operettas. Why, people ask, should a company be considered admirable because it looks good on the bottom line? Is a person to be admired because he or she has money in the bank? It is not just that a corporation, like a person, may have made money in questionable ways. The uneasiness about profit goes deeper. Irving Kristol once declared that while only a saint or a snob would dismiss lightly the important role of the profit motive, to call it the only measure of a business flies in the face of human understanding. "Who wants to live in a society in which selfishness and self-seeking are celebrated as primary virtues? Such a society is unfit for human habitation. . . . Businessmen desperately try to defend their vocation as honorable because profitable. Without realizing it, they are standing Horatio Alger on his head."[4]

In fact, a number of business leaders with unquestionable credentials have reached a similar conclusion on their own. For instance:

> For a long time people believed that the only purpose of industry was to make a profit. They were wrong. Its purpose is the general welfare. —Henry Ford

> We do not see Xerox as solely a profit-making institution. I don't want to minimize profits . . . but I must emphasize that we regard Xerox as a social institution as well as a business institution. —C. Peter McColough (chief executive of Xerox)

But if profit is not the only objective of the corporation, it is still a vital need. Constitutionalism could not be justified in government if, let us say, it destroyed the power to tax. Neither could constitutionalism be justified in the corporation if it destroyed profits. The Founding Fathers did not see the Bill of Rights as the downfall of government but as one of its most important processes. Similarly, we must be able to conceive of employee rights as a sound and productive part of the profit-making process or we cannot make a strong case for them. After all, profit is far more than a reward. Many college economics instructors and some business spokesmen keep calling it that, but though they may call it a reward three million times, that does not make it true.

When we were children and our mothers helped us put up a table and sell lemonade to passers-by on hot summer days, we counted the nickels and dimes afterward and proudly announced how much money we had made. This was our profit, our reward for being enterprising.

However, in the grown-up world of auto makers, oil companies, chain stores, and other big businesses, profit is a different thing. Out of habit, people may call it a "reward," because of course much of it does go to stockholders as a payback on their investment, and many stockholders get back more than they invested. But in reality, profit is not a reward. In all our major industries where there is competition, profit is a *cost*. It is just as much a cost as employee salaries and the water bill. If a profit is not earned, or if it is not large enough, the company will be unable to raise needed funds on the stock market or borrow from banks. Who wants to invest in a company that can't pay dividends, or lend to a firm that can't pay back the loan on time?

Therefore, we must be able to assure ourselves that profits will not be a casualty of employee rights—at least, until some superrace finds a way to keep corporations dynamic without the help of leaders and equity investors. As Peter Drucker once said, if archangels sat in the corporate board room instead of businessmen, they would still have to be concerned with profitability.

There are three reasons that employee constitutionalism is not likely to threaten the capitalistic bottom line.

First, during recent years several U.S. corporations have expanded the rights of employees, as we shall see in later chapters. None of these companies paid for their idealism by going out of business. In fact, they happen to be quite profitable enterprises. It is true that none of them went so far as to establish rights of speech, conscience, privacy, *and* due process. Their efforts have been limited to just part of the potential list. But if employee constitutionalism were death for profits, one would think the bottom line would leak at least a little bit as a result of management's boldness. There is no evidence such harm has been done.

Furthermore, quite a few companies in Sweden and Norway have established a variety of employee rights. These companies have been holding their own nicely in world competition.

Second, as business leaders themselves have said tirelessly, profit is produced not by mirrors, management, or machines but by people—people in their infinite variety and sacredness, in their complex personalities and irrational desires. Employee constitutionalism is a way for people of this real world to express and relate themselves to the work of the organization. If there is such a thing as "mental health" for a collective of people, then constitutionalism should be a tonic, for it is antisuppressive, antischizophrenic.

Morever, employee constitutionalism is a way of reducing the excessive dependence of subordinates on their supervisors. It means that the employee who wants to assert his or her ethical and moral standards is not going to suffer for doing so. Civil liberties and due process mean greater freedom for employees—not perfect freedom, perhaps, but more than they have had in the past.

Third, giving employees a psychological stake in capitalism could be just as valuable as giving them an economic stake in it. During recent years, one plan after another has been advanced for giving employees a financial interest in corporate performance—Kelso plans, employee

stock ownership plans (now encouraged by federal legislation), and others. Is it not also important to develop employee commitment to the ideas, ideals, and humanity of an
enterprise? Pope John XXIII wrote:

> Like our predecessors, we are convinced of the legitimacy of
> the workers' ambition to take part in the life of the undertaking
> in which they are employed. . . . We consider . . . that work-
> ers must be given an active part to play in the management of
> the concern in which they are employed, whether that concern
> be public or private.[5]

THE AGE OF AFFLUENT INDIVIDUALISM

Actually, the most important relationship may be not between employee rights and capitalism but between employee rights and individualism. After all, without a broad
socio-cultural basis of personal enterprise and ambition,
capitalism would never work.

There is a mistaken tendency to relate the employee
rights movement to alienation, division of labor, exploitation
of the workforce, and matters of that sort. This view sells the
movement short. The desire for increased civil liberties in
employment is more than a work phenomenon. It is more
than a reaction to perceived injustice or inequality. In fact,
it is even more than an economic event.

Employee rights is part of a new wave of individualism
that has spread across society. The new individualism is
more qualitative than quantitative. It is fed by lengthening
leisure hours, modern education with its stress on individual attitudes and interpretation, moral relativism, burgeon-
ing communication, technological profusion, and social af-
fluence. Let me offer a simple example.

As so many parents and employers know all too well,
younger workers don't feel under the old-time pressure to
stay continuously at work or "prove themselves" as soon as
possible to their employers. When I completed my school-

ing in 1949, I was out of work for several weeks—very nearly an economic disaster for me, and a traumatic experience, too. Recently my son spent his first year after college graduation doing odd jobs in order to save up for a trip to Europe. Only after that did he plan to start a serious work career. These days there is more money to go around, there is unemployment compensation, there is the "stay loose" culture of the young, and last but not least, there is the pill, which means that a young couple can wait to get married and, after that, wait to have children until they are good and ready. Feeling less dependent on employers, young employees are more willing to march to their own drummer instead of the hierarchy's.

Individualism today must not be measured against the individualism of the past, for it is different in quality. The affluent individualism of today doesn't entertain Horatio Alger–like dreams of becoming a president or a railroad tycoon. It dreams of expressing oneself, of being a free, unfettered, unbeholden, hobby-loving, vacation-taking member of a good company and liver of the good life; and it values belonging—not so much belonging to God, Mammon, or *Who's Who*, as in the Age of Alger, as belonging to the community and the regional web of life. Yesterday's "rugged individual" sought security through accomplishment and estate building; today's affluent individual seeks security through affiliation with co-workers, neighbors, social clubs, sports fans, and the environment. His motto is not "Onward and upward" but "O Brother Man" (inscription on a sundial at the University of Virginia).

The same businessmen, government officials, and others who lament the "decline of individualism" resent the stiffening resistance of employees to "taking a lot of crap" from management, and the growing proclivity to speak out in criticism of a company that does not appear to be working in the ethical, social, and environmental interests of a community. These latter activities, though individualistic in the eyes of affluent employees, are not defined as individualism by many senior bosses. Why?

At least some of the explanation lies in our business heritage. During the sixteenth, seventeenth, and eighteenth centuries, business was seen as an agent of the state. Industry and commerce were seen as enhancing the greater glory of France, let us say, or of England, or of Spain. To free himself of bondage to the state, the businessman seized on the individualistic values expressed by intellectuals of the Renaissance and Reformation. He maintained that if a business could meet the needs of the state and customers, that was fine. However, the main reason for its existence was the pursuit of private gain and satisfaction.

This is why, explains Ross A. Webber, "businessmen in confrontation sing the praises of the free man as an individual—his ability to make his way in the world, to conquer nature and promote his own welfare and the interests of humanity at the same time."[6]

John Locke, the seventeenth-century English philosopher, saw private property as the essential guarantor of individual rights. His philosophy (along with Adam Smith's a century later) couldn't have been better calculated to help business people rationalize and legitimize the pursuit of commercial profit. The Lockean emphasis on property has been useful to this day, though for an ever-contracting circle of people. George Lodge, who has devoted considerable study to the roots of business values, explains:

> For some people, the individualistic drive for the possession of property and for its full exploitation may remain a motivating factor. But for most of us, the motivating force has been vitiated by the increasing difficulty of such individualistic entrepreneurial pursuit in the face of huge organizations, the increasing conflicts between that pursuit and the community's social and ecological needs, and the fact that as a practical matter few men or women have the opportunity to possess that sort of property which insures political independence and freedom.[7]

Lodge believes that *communitarian* values—by which he refers to fulfillment occurring through "participation in an organic social process" and the exercise of rights of membership—are replacing nineteenth-century and early twentieth-century individualism. His choice of terms is appealing, for the word *individualism* may have become so rigidly defined in the old sense that it cannot grow resiliently and take on new meanings.

However, we are today witnessing so much more expression of personal preference, so much more rejection of bondage to bosses of any sort, and such adamant resistance to letting business, political, and church leaders act as our surrogates in value formation and policy thinking, that the concept of individualism may in actuality be better fulfilled today—for most people—than it ever was. Much of the dissidence in the marketplace, workplace, campus, and home is coming from individuals and small groups. Although stimulated by publicity about other dissident individuals and groups, the activities generally are not coordinated, the groups are dissimilarly constituted, and the activists use different words and terms to articulate their needs and goals. Time and time again, claims that they were "organized" by communist, socialist, or foreign powers have been proved utterly false.

I am not now endorsing or approving the dissidents. I wish only to point out that they represent an intensity and profusion of individualism that was unknown in most of Western history.

WORK—MONEY ISN'T EVERYTHING

Another trend that has given enormous impetus to the employee rights movement is the rise of the so-called "knowledge worker."

The more knowledge and skill a job requires of the worker, the greater the tendency for the worker to relate the purpose of his job to the perceived needs of society. The human-turned-robot who flips panels on a drill press line day after day brings little knowledge to his job, takes little out, and has no good reason to think about anything except his paycheck. But when a person brings training, know-how, and any degree of professional skill to his work, it becomes natural to look more inquiringly at the role and operation of the organization. For the employee meets from time to time with others like him and "talks shop." He or she reads trade magazines and professional journals which, at the same time that they help him expand his knowledge, explain to him what other knowledge workers in other areas are doing and thinking. Questions of social responsibility, organizational ethics, consumerism, and fair treatment come up in every-day conversation and perplex him.

Not so many generations ago, knowledge workers were a minority on the payrolls of business, government, and other public organizations. The philosophy of "management knows best" and "hired hands should put up or shut up" made some sense then, not because employees were stupid but becuase they had little occasion to relate their own nar-row jobs to the wider world of work. By contrast, knowledge workers are in the majority in business and government to-day, and their majority is swelling. Some of them, especially the formal professionals, such as chemists and physicists, are said to feel more loyalty to their professions than to their employers.

For knowledge workers, there must be more in work than a paycheck. There must also be some satisfaction that what one is doing is worthwhile from society's standpoint. As Littlefair and other philosophers have pointed out, a job must be seen not as a burden but as a means of contributing to society, of participating, of belonging. Money is overem-phasized when it becomes the symbol and justification of a job, for then it divorces us from the reality of our related-ness. If all we work for is money, then the job becomes a symbol exclusively of taking; the giving possibilities are left out and, with them, the potential of work for satisfying our ego needs.

Are civil liberties a threat to private enterprise? If private enterprise depends mostly on top-down obedience and control, yes; if private enterprise depends more on initiative and esprit de corps, no. During a meeting with some management trainees at Radcliffe College several years ago, Harvard law professor Zechariah Chafee, Jr., noted that employee rights do help to bring important information and judgments to light—but that is not the only gain. Rights also create devotion to the enterprise. They create the kind of spirit which leads a person to think, "I am a small part of my company, but my company is a big part of me."

The belief that work should be ego satisfying has excited employees' desires to speak out when they see their organizations engaging in activities that seem socially, morally, or legally reprehensible. This important question is the subject of the next chapter.

NOTES

1. Duncan E. Littlefair, *The Glory Within You* (Philadelphia: Westminster Press, 1973), p. 179. The chapter was drawn from sermons given by Littlefair during the 1950s and early 1960s.
2. Address to Association of General Counsel, Dearborn, Michigan, October 14, 1974.
3. Peter Drucker, *Management* (New York: Harper & Row, 1974), Chapter 29.
4. Irving Kristol, "Horatio Alger and Profits," *Wall Street Journal*, July 11, 1974.
5. Pope John XXIII, Encyclical *Mater et Magistra*, 1962.
6. Ross A. Webber, "Advertising and Product Responsibility," *Business and Society*, Autumn 1966, p. 25.
7. George C. Lodge, *Harvard Today*, 1972, p. 7.

5
BOTTOM-UP
ETHICS

In public agencies and businesses directed by executives with high ethical standards and good control systems, it is relatively easy to police lower-echelon employees who step out of line. For instance, IBM publishes a fairly detailed code of conduct for managers, asks them to study and sign it, and is very tough on violators. Everyone in the company knows that the corporate heads "really mean it" when they say they expect these ethical rules to be observed scrupulously. And because work performance is reported up the line so well, only the most vulpine and lucky employee has a chance of getting away with a violation.

The key is the management information system. When the top executive wants to reach down and find out what is going on, he has some marvelous tools, thanks to modern skills in reporting and to the computer. When Louis Cabot, head of the Cabot Corporation, was elected to the board of the Penn Central in the 1960s, one of the first things he did was ask the chief executive for certain types of information on managerial activities. To Cabot, it was inconceivable that management could expect ethical performance if operations were conducted in a tenebrous atmosphere. When the chief executive refused to provide the reports requested, Cabot resigned. As he was to learn later, there were good reasons that some of Penn Central's people did not want the board to know what was going on. There was in that organization what the poet John Keats would have called an "inhuman dearth of noble natures," and the company was being bled dry.

But what if the organization heads themselves, or their close subordinates, are engaged in sleight-of-hand activities? Obviously, then, pressure for ethical improvement is not going to come from the top down. It must come from the bottom up—or from the law outside.

Here is where the rub comes. Unlike the top people looking down, lower-level people cannot demand information about the behavior of top management. However, they may learn of wrongdoing, see it, smell it, be ordered to cooperate in carrying it out. Yet they cannot speak out or report it without jeopardizing their jobs.

To add to the irony, employees at the middle and lower levels often possess higher ethical standards than the leaders do. When this happens, it does not come about by sheer coincidence. As any reader of Shakespeare knows, ethical standards may be easy victims of ambition and power, which typically sit with the top official in his or her sarcophagus of tubular steel and lighted glass. Unexposed to the terrible temptations of high office, middle- and lower-level employees may be able to maintain the sounder perspective that their bosses lose. Although this is not always the case, it happens often enough. Watergate is only the most dramatic evidence of ethical standards reasserting themselves from the bottom up and from the outside in.

In decades past employees would have been considered out of order to blow the whistle on top management wrongdoing. But this attitude is disappearing. More and more Americans, however modest their material achievements, are unwilling to let their leaders do their ethical thinking for them. (In many other parts of the world the same trend is evident.) And so they are willing to challenge organization heads and their satraps who appear to be engaged in illegal, immoral, or irresponsible activity. The record contains abundant evidence that bottom-up ethics can and does work, even under very disadvantageous circumstances.

Two U.S. senators who can testify to the existence of motivated whistle-blowers are William Proxmire of Wisconsin and Edward Kennedy of Massachusetts. From 1970 to 1973 Proxmire worked on behalf of A. Ernest Fitzgerald, the Pentagon employee who was sacked after testifying, against the wishes of his bosses in the Air Force, about huge cost overruns for the giant cargo plane, the C5A. Although at one time the Justice Department as well as the Air Force seemed bent on keeping Fitzgerald blackballed for "committing the truth," Proxmire and other officials finally succeeded in getting him reinstated.

Kennedy sponsored hearings in 1975 to publicize the cause of government employees who spoke out against illegal or immoral actions in their agencies. One outcome of these hearings was Senate bill 1210, proposed to protect such employees by giving them direct access to the courts in order to "redress agency retaliation against them arising out of proper disclosures of information." (The bill has not yet been reported out of committee.) Among the cases reported at the Kennedy hearings were those of:

—Rudy Frank, suspended by the Office of Economic Opportunity for releasing data showing misexpenditures of day care funds, and reinstated after a Freedom of Information lawsuit and union arbitration.

—Jacqueline Varrett, an employee of the Food and Drug Administration who disclosed data on the dangers of cyclamates and was penalized by what came close to official shunning, in the Mennonite sense of that term.

—Mary Lepper, who challenged the propriety of equal employment opportunity processes at her agency, Health, Education, and Welfare, and was harassed and penalized by her bosses as a result.

—Sandra Kramer and Valerie Koster, employees of the Indian Health Service, who sent a letter to President Nixon about the shocking conditions at Shiprock Hospital, were fired, and reinstated after the Kennedy committee aired their cases.

—John Moffat, an employee of the Internal Revenue Service who spoke out about improper expenditure of funds at his agency, was relieved of his usual responsibilities, and, following the committee hearings, transferred to a job equivalent to the old one but (at his request) in a different city.

Two things are worth noting about the experience of Senators Proxmire and Kennedy with whistle-blowers.

First, because both senators are engaged in numerous other activities, they cannot possibly attend to more than a small fraction of the cases they might otherwise turn up in their investigations. The examples reported are but the tip of an iceberg.

Second, the whistle-blowers were up against terrible odds. They were risking their jobs, friends, security, and peace of mind by speaking out, and they knew it. Taking on a well-informed, well-organized, affluent, and powerful hierarchy, they knew in advance that they probably would be picked off like Custer's army. For just a brief sampling of the price of whistle-blowing, consider the following:

—Ernest Fitzgerald, the Pentagon employee who reported the C5A cost overruns and got dumped, was in litigation limbo for five years before he could return to his desk—and when he did return he did not receive his full back pay. According to Senator Kennedy, sympathetic lawyers donated a hundred thousand dollars worth of time to his case.

—Sandra Kramer and Valerie Koster, the Indian Health Service employees who got scalped after reporting the ugly conditions at Shiprock Hospital, were reinstated after the Kennedy Committee hearings, but they were transferred against their wishes to another station, Kennedy reported.

—Henry Durham, an executive for Lockheed who struggled fruitlessly within the company to resolve various irregularities associated with C5A production before taking the matter to Senator Proxmire, suffered for six years—and at last report was still suffering—because of his "disloyalty." Not only the company but town citizens and the local church were snubbing him.

—In May 1969, Michael Holodnak, a skilled worker of the Avco-Lycoming Division of Avco Corporation in Stratford, Connecticut, was fired for publishing an article critical of the company and the union. (This case will be discussed in more detail in Chapter 6.) Five years after the firing, in 1974, the U.S. District Court of Connecticut finally handed down a decision in his favor.[1] But it was a Pyrrhic victory. He was awarded $9,113 in back pay (obviously only a portion of what he would have earned in five years) and $10,000 of the $30,000 punitive damages he sought; his attorneys' fees were ordered to be paid by the company and union. The court decided against reinstating him in his job. Suggesting the severe emotional and physical costs of waiting out five years of litigation without a job, the court noted that his "physical condition, observed at trial, makes it doubtful that he is physically capable of returning to doing the work he had been doing."

Many more such examples could be supplied. Numerous examples could also be supplied of whistle-blowers whose actions have led to official investigations of companies and other organizations. For instance, Thomas M. Howard, a financial executive of Cenco, a Chicago concern, went to the SEC in 1975 with information about the company's fraudulent statements of sales and profits. Gulf Oil Corporation's $12.3 million political slush fund was exposed with the help of two employees. The imbroglio at Southwestern Bell, charged with political payoffs and wiretapping, broke in the fall of 1974 as the result of reports from insiders. Much of what columnist Jack Anderson revealed in 1972 about the shady side of ITT apparently came from an employee who slipped him internal memos. In the 1960s a defective brake scandal at B. F. Goodrich came to light when one of the company's data analysts went to the FBI. The Equity Funding, Investors Overseas Services, and other schemes were dug out partly by insiders during the early 1970s. According to *Time* magazine in 1972, Robert Rowen, a technician at Pacific Gas and Electric, filed forty-nine charges with the Atomic Energy Commission alleging deliberate violation by the company of government safety regulations regarding the handling of radioactive waste. In *Blowing the Whistle: Dissent in the Public Interest*,[2] Charles Peters and Taylor Branch present several case studies of government employees who revealed abuses or deceptions by their employer organizations.

Of course, the skeptic is quick to point out that such cases are extremely small in number compared to the potential that exists. For every active whistle-blower, there must be many thousands who could have played the role but didn't. It should be remembered, however, that this trend is in its infancy. The amazing thing is that it exists. To paraphrase Samuel Johnson's answer to the man who asked him what he thought of a certain woman preacher, the whistle-blower is like a dog who walks on his hind legs—it doesn't much matter how well it is done or by how many, what is remarkable is that it is done at all.

FOR WHOM THE WHISTLE BLOWS

Years ago there reportedly flew over the Chicago Tribune tower a flag with the motto, "My country right or wrong, but my country." On the walls of a leading textile manufacturer there used to be posted the slogan, "Organization above self." As official pronouncements, such sayings are considered old-fashioned now, but the attitude represented is quite alive and robust. From the time we are children we are taught to value "playing on the team." As Kenneth D. Walters observes, the whistle-blower is often seen in the spirit of Judas Iscariot, not Martin Luther. He quotes a statement by Peters and Branch that "in fact, whistle blowing is severely hampered by the image of its most famous historical model, Judas Iscariot. Martin Luther seems to be about the only figure of note to make much headway with public opinion after doing an inside job on a corrupt organization."[3]

An executive I know, after being told about Senator Kennedy's bill S. 1210, remarked disdainfully that a right-to-rat law would not make ratting less obnoxious.

Can the employee rights movement make headway against such a deeply ingrained attitude? As long as the public feels, like my friend, that the employer organization is the only legitimate object of an employee's loyalty, the answer must be "very little." But it seems clear that the public does not regard an organization in that light. For at least two decades there has been a conspicuous trend in favor of multiple loyalties—to the community, to the nation, to morality, to the environment, as well as to individual corporations and public agencies. In short, the whistle-blower can value loyalty as much as anyone does, only his or her loyalty is pluralistic.

Another hurdle is organizational discipline. As Christopher Stone points out, whistle-blowing threatens "the hierarchical principles and role-playing niceties upon which all organizations are built."[4] Anyone who has listened to employees talk in many companies knows how deeply they fear and respect hierarchical power. "This is a totalitarian government, buddy, and we don't ever forget it"—this sort of statement characterizes employee thought in many more organizations than it does not. Although it may be true that employees often exaggerate the requirements of discipline, fancying their bosses as more Draconian than they really are, the threat of retaliation is quite real.

For example, when Fitzgerald testified on C5A cost overruns, it is reported that two aides to President Nixon, Pat Buchanan and Clark Mollenhoff, counseled against his dismissal. (Sixty Congressmen also opposed the firing.) But Alexander P. Butterfield, deputy assistant secretary of the Air Force, later to become head of the Federal Aviation Administration and the man who revealed that Nixon's conversations had been taped, disagreed. In a memo to presidential assistant H. R. Haldeman, he advised that "we should let him bleed, for a while, at least." When Fitzgerald named Butterfield a defendant in a suit alleging a conspiracy to deprive him of his constitutional rights, Butterfield conceded that "let him bleed" was a poor choice of words. "I meant," he said, "let him cry, let him suffer, for at least a while." Butterfield was not ashamed of his memo, for while he considered Fitzgerald a top-notch cost expert, he believed he went out of bounds in expressing his views to people other than his superiors.[5]

From a psychological standpoint, it is fascinating that employees' antagonism toward superiors often seems to become transformed into antagonism toward outsiders when their organization comes under attack or suspicion. Just as many internecine quarrels in a family or nation are shelved in times of emergency, so the solidarity of an organization may grow when, say, a public investigation of it is launched, or a Ralph Nader points an accusing finger at it. This common tendency has so impressed Professor Robert G. Vaughn that, to counteract it, he suggests penalties on government employees who fail to report accurately information that is demanded by public investigators under the Freedom of Information act.[6]

On the other side of the coin is the desire to please superiors. When Richardson-Merrell was testing its new drug, MER/29, which later harmed some users and led to the company's indictment for criminal negligence, lab experiments revealed the drug's harmful effects. But so anxious was one laboratory to tell management what it hoped to hear that it reported the condition of a certain animal test group as "good, except for loss of hair and sight."[7]

How serious an obstacle is the prejudice against "ratting?" Probably it is the highest hurdle in making constitutionalism effective in organizations. But while it would be idealistic to hope that most or even many employees will ever dare to challenge hierarchical discipline, it should not be unrealistic to expect the small minority of potential dissidents to increase gradually, as it seems to have been doing in recent decades.

Moreover, so long as the whistle-blowers have the dogged determination of the Fitzgeralds, Holodnaks, and others, it should not be necessary for their numbers to be large in order to put the brakes on a substantial amount of managerial and white-collar crime. Here we might remember what football star Archie Griffin was told by his high school football coach, who disagreed with all those who felt Griffin's small size would keep him out of big-time college football. "It's not the size of the dog in the fight," said the mentor, "but the size of the fight in the dog that counts."

SECRECY AND OPENNESS

So long as companies and public agencies are "tight little islands" known to the public only by their exports of goods and services, annual picnics, and press releases, sleight of hand is bound to be more common than in open organizations. Isolated and insulated from public opinion, the unprincipled strong man is tempted to hold to a double standard of morality. One is reminded of William Golding's chilling tale *Lord of the Flies,* wherein the bullying Jack Merridew terrorizes all who are marooned on an island, succeeding finally in establishing his evil ethic beyond challenge. Only when rescuers from the outside world arrive can morality be reasserted.

In short, the need is to build bridges between corporate and public organizations and the societal mainland. Else how can public opinion be brought to bear to check managers who may engage in practices that run counter to the law, moral standards, or the public interest?

Although secrecy is essential in many types of organizational activities—research and development, product plans, service innovations, marketing campaigns, and so forth—a line needs to be drawn between areas such as these and areas where the public is entitled to know because of the possibility of adverse effects on its legitimate interest.

Americans' sense of community is enlarging as a result of

increasing interdependence, travel, and communication. The conviction is growing that employers are small, society is great. The employee who swallows his objections to immoral or illegal practices he sees going on, out of loyalty to the boss or the department, is disloyal to stockholders, consumers, and the public at large, for both directly and indirectly every sizable company, college, and public agency influences the quality of life. The whistle-blower sounds an alert for the public as well as for the organizational staff. To paraphrase John Donne's famous line, "Never send to know for whom the whistle blows; it blows for thee."

WHY OUTSIDE-IN SWINGS FAIL

When a golfer uses an outside-in swing, cutting across the ball, his shot usually curves to the right and lands in the rough, or maybe in the woods or local water hole. When outside investigators, whether district attorneys or Ralph Nader types, attempt to invade the ethical miasma of a wayward agency or corporation, the outside-in swing may fail again. They may get near the target but not near enough.

For one thing, managerial and white-collar crime is not conspicuous. It is marked by no red flag. It is not ugly, repulsive, or violent, as common crimes are. Early in the century sociologist E. A. Ross observed:

> The stealings and slayings that lurk in the complexities of our social relations are not deeds of the dive, the dark alley, the lonely road, and the midnight hour. They require no nocturnal prowling with muffled step and bated breath, no weapon or offer of violence. . . . The modern high-powered dealer of woe wears immaculate linen, carries a silk hat and a lighted cigar, sins with a serene soul, leagues or months from the evil he causes. . . . The hurt passes into that vague mass, the "public," and is there lost to view. . . . Often there are no victims.[8]

Another obstacle is the difficulty of detection. When the wayward corpocrat doctors financial statements or falsifies research reports, no one is likely to be looking over his shoulder. Moreover, he operates in a sea of organizational secrecy. The whole corporation, agency, or administration is impervious to the prying of the outside world, not just his operation alone. If silence were a wall, most companies and public agencies would be ringed like a medieval castle. Publicity releases and press conferences may give a superficial appearance to the contrary, but of course they carry only the information management wants outsiders to hear.

Even when law enforcement officials do smell a foul wind from a wayward corporation and march in to investigate, they may find nothing. Consider the millions of dollars in bribes reportedly paid in recent years by Lockheed, United Brands, Exxon, and other large corporations to foreign governments, or the enormous sums allegedly swindled in the Home-Stake Production, Mattel, and other publicized cases. Reading about such infractions, we are impressed by the boldness of the perpetrators. But in the labyrinthine accounts of a large corporation, a payoff of $1 million or less may be as hard to detect as a gnat at night.

The outside-in approach tends to slice into the rough for still another reason. Substantive questions can be raised about the adequacy of legal punishment of managerial crime. Does the threat of fine or prison really deter the potential wrongdoer? In his or her planning, there is at least a short period of high profit before the bottom drops out, and experience gives us reason to wonder if that initial payoff doesn't loom larger in the wrongdoer's scheme of things than the later reversal. Or, he may optimistically figure that he and his bank account will be well beyond reach of the law by the time the crime is discovered.

What is more, the punishment may not really hurt when it is inflicted. As has been pointed out many times, the architects and executors of illegal payoffs, financial manipulations, and other schemes seldom undergo traumatic experiences after being sentenced. As for penalizing the organization collectively, the courts have been urged to slug companies with far higher fines, as a means of making managerial shenanigans a common danger for all employees to guard against, but that course is not likely to change things much. The $7 million in fines assessed against Ford Motor Company in 1972 because of serious violations of the Environmental Protection Act, the $80,000 assessment against Richardson Merrell for producing a hazardous cholesterol-repressing drug (MER/29), and similar penalties are paltry sums for sizable corporations. Even if such fines were to be increased, there is little evidence that managers would be intimidated. Their own compensation tends to be unaffected by ups and downs in the corporate treasury.

Besides, judges hesitate to assess crippling damages. In the Richardson-Merrell case, Judge Henry Friendly feared that a severer penalty might "end the business life of a concern that has wrought much good in the past and might otherwise have continued to do so in the future, with many innocent stockholders suffering extinction of their investments from a single management sin."[9]

A significant innovation in legal and economic thought is the idea that the decision-making processes in wayward companies should be altered so that temptation can be better avoided. Most companies abide by the law. Why cannot checks and balances of the sort these companies use successfully to thwart wrongdoers be injected into the minority of companies that get into trouble?

In *Where the Law Ends*[10] Christopher Stone offers an elegant series of arguments for this approach. Almost all procapitalist economists and legislators believe in treating the corporation's inner processes as a "black box," to be influenced only indirectly by such external threats as court-imposed fines, restrictive statutes, new regulatory commissions and the countervailing power of unions, consumer groups, and stockholders. And that is the way Adam Smith would have it if he were here to defend the philosophy of *The Wealth of Nations*. But Stone thinks otherwise. Public officials must stick their hands into the decision-making machinery itself, he says. We need more straightforward "intrusions" into the corporation's decision structure.

When a company is found guilty of negligence, irresponsibility, or illegal behavior, a federal court or agency can "inject" officials charged with correcting the abusive tendencies. In 1974 a federal court in Washington, D.C. ordered Mattel, a toy manufacturer some of whose executives had been playing fraudulent games with stockholders, to appoint two new directors to its board; the directors had to be outsiders, approved by both the court and the SEC. In addition, the court required the company to set up several committees charged with investigating and overseeing certain activities in the company that no one theretofore had controlled.

In short, by changing the way in which the company was managed, the court hoped to improve its collective "conscience" and also eliminate some of the excuses innocent managers had had for not knowing what was going on. While few such actions have been taken yet, because of the distaste—in keeping with Adam Smith's doctrines—for interfering with management, Stone sees no reason that courts could not follow the precedent much more often.

At least a few federal judges have agreed. In April 1976, a federal court ordered that three outside directors be elected to the board of Lockheed, which was then in disrepute because of repeated revelations about its secret political payoffs to obtain contracts.

In a *Harvard Business Review* article, Stone proposes "in-house probation officers," or limited public directors to help clean up demonstrated delinquency in management.[11] Such officers are needed because "a giant corporation can put between itself and the law's taunts a far thicker skin than can the ordinary human." Public directors could be court-appointed or proposed by regulatory agencies. Stone suggests that special directors be designated to receive bad news requiring an internal corporate investigation. He doesn't think this step would reduce the board room to a "factionalist brawl," and in any case "some new degree of factionalism would be preferable to the present degree of clubbiness."

Such approaches could be very useful. Because of certain shortcomings, however, they do not obviate the need for whistle-blowing. They tend to close the barn door after the horses have fled—or, at least, after some of the horses have fled. Hence their deterrent value is reduced. In addition, they share the weakness of having to wait for the crime to be reported somehow, or to become so tumescent that outsiders can see it.

Another shortcoming is that courts and law enforcement agencies have limited abilities to supervise changes in an errant organization's decision making. If the need for such supervision arose only now and then, fine; but if numerous cases were to land in the laps of the courts and regulatory agencies, they would find themselves overwhelmed.

In addition, there is the philosophical argument that the country already has too much government intervention. Former U.S. Senator Sam Ervin of North Carolina complained that "the federal bureaucracy has become like the third curse of Moses—a suffocating plague of frogs brought forth from out of where they belong into the villages and the very houses of the people." The Sam Ervins of society are not likely to be pleased at the thought of new agencies and appropriations so that government can order changes to be made in the internal operations of derelict companies and other organizations.

Of course, whistle-blowers will not bring the millennium, either. Their motives range from putrid to pure. While some are impelled by an acute sense of justice or public concern, others are like ants longing to be grasshoppers. Nevertheless, opening the way for correction from the bottom up is sound in principle. Combined with other new approaches, such as those mentioned, it could sharpen efforts both to deter and apprehend wrongdoers.

In addition, stockholders and the public will benefit financially every time a fraudulent scheme or cover-up is aborted at an early stage. Consider a concrete and well-documented example: Because a middle-management cover-up of a defective plane brake produced by B. F.

Goodrich Company was successful for a long period, the U.S. Air Force, which was Goodrich's customer for the brake, paid exorbitant costs, the company was subjected to bad publicity at government hearings, and Goodrich's profits for two years were reduced. This series of losses was unnecessary. Early in the story, several Goodrich employees wanted very much to blow the whistle. However, they did not dare do so because of the near certainty that their immediate bosses would retaliate by firing them. Had they felt better protected, they were prepared to go to top management and tell their story. A costly and scandalous sequence of events would have been avoided.[12]

Critics of employee rights carp about the expense of allowing whistle-blowing. But what about the exorbitant costs of silence?

NOTES

1. *Holodnak* v. *AVCO Corporation, Avco-Lycoming Division, et al.,* Civil Action No. B-15 (1974) U.S. District Court, Connecticut.
2. Charles Peters and Taylor Branch, *Blowing the Whistle: Dissent in the Public Interest* (New York: Praeger, 1972), p. 4.
3. Kenneth D. Walters, "Your Employees' Right to Blow the Whistle," *Harvard Business Review,* July-August 1975, p. 27.
4. Christopher D. Stone, *Where the Law Ends* (New York: Harper & Row, 1975), p. 215.
5. *New York Times,* March 26, 1971.
6. Robert Vaughn, "The Freedom of Information Act and Vaughn v. Rosen: Some Personal Comments," *The American University Law Review* 23 (Summer 1974): 877.
7. Stone, p. 207.
8. E. A. Ross, *Sin and Society* (Boston: Houghton Mifflin Co., 1907), p. 9.
9. Stone, p. 181.
10. Stone, pp. 184–227.
11. Christopher D. Stone, "Public Directors Merit a Try," *Harvard Business Review,* March-April 1976, p. 20.
12. For a complete account of the Goodrich airbrake story, see Kermit Vandivier, "Why Should My Conscience Bother Me?" in *In the Name of Profit* by Robert L. Heilbroner and others (New York: Doubleday & Company, Inc., 1972), pp. 3–31.

PART III

Needed Rights

Freedom from something is not enough. It should also be freedom for something. Freedom is not safety but opportunity.

—Zechariah Chafee, Jr.

6

LOOSENING
THE GAG
ON
EMPLOYEES

"Give me the liberty to know, to utter, and to argue freely according to conscience, above all liberties," wrote John Milton in his treatise *Areopagitica*. Of all freedoms, speech and press are not only the most satisfying but also the most powerful, for inevitably they lead to the creation of other freedoms. In view of this chain reaction effect, it is no wonder that a right to free speech is resisted more stubbornly by management than any other concession it can make to employees.

It is not true, however, that management's principal fear is exposure of its miscalculations, errors in judgment, or wrongdoing. This possibility may make a few executives squirm, but it is not the major preoccupation. After all, in most cases management has thought through its plans, programs, and policies more thoroughly than any dissident employee group could ever hope to do. Moreover, most managements are as anxious as anyone to stamp out illegal and unethical shenanigans. When charges of political bribes and illegal wiretaps were made aginst Southwestern Bell, following T. O. Gravitt's suicide note in late 1974, John De-Butts, head of the Bell System, was the first to press for complete investigation and corrective action.

Nor is it true that fear of adverse publicity is the key to

management intractability. Naturally this is a factor. Napoleon said he feared three newspapers more than a hundred thousand bayonets, and many executives would fear three newspapers reporting the criticisms of a dissident employee more than a $100,000 drain from the bottom line of the profit statement. But even this is not the dominating obsession, especially as management gets more used to the idea that its actions affecting the community are fit subjects for public discussion.

What management fears most of all is the perceived threat to the hierarchy of power. Why did Pope Urban VIII go to such lengths to persecute Galileo for his demonstrations that the earth goes around the sun, instead of vice versa? After all, an earlier scientist, Copernicus, had already proposed that the old Ptolemaic notion was false, so Galileo's conclusions weren't new, only his proofs. Moreover, when he was summoned for final condemnation, he was seventy years old and sick. Yet Galileo's dissidence and his reluctance to compromise so disturbed the Catholic Church that the Holy Office of the Inquisition worked on its case for twenty-two years before the trial finally began in 1633.

It was not the challenge to the Church's doctrines that Pope Urban feared so much, but the challenge to its authority. The same obsession dominates the thinking of many leaders and executives in business, government, and other institutions. They worry that management's ability to manage will be weakened, that a fissure will be created which will cause the whole pyramid to tumble down. They see the many restrictions imposed on them by collective bargaining laws, safety laws, equal employment opportunity regulations, environmental agencies, the countervailing power of consumerism, and so forth. No one of these by itself is dangerous. But, like Gulliver, management sees so many little restraints being wound around it that *cumulatively* they could be incapacitating. Mightn't a limited right to employee free speech be the most debilitating restriction of all?

When CBS televised an hour-long program on Phillips Petroleum, in December 1973, it described the strict discipline of this great oil company's 35,000 employees. When an employee deviated from the unwritten company rules about dress, manners, gasoline station patronage, or other behavior, he was penalized quickly and harshly. "The rest of the pack turns aginst him," William W. Keeler, the chief executive, told the interviewer. A lower-echelon employee interviewed by CBS explained in more detail: "It's a simple trade-off. If you want them to feed, clothe, and maintain you and keep you in health and provide you with all the sustenance of life that you want, you simply have to cooperate with them and conform with their rules and conform to their policies."

Reviewing the program in the *New York Times*, John J. O'Connor wrote that at Phillips there was "a direct ratio between the extent of an individual's ambitions and the pressure for conformity."[1]

This "simple trade-off" is commonly believed to be not only fair but essential to efficient organization, and it applies with particular force to the question of free speech and press. Until recently, it was difficult to disprove the belief. However, evidence now exists that casts a question mark over the authoritarian doctrine.

—At a New England electronics plant of Corning Glass, executives encourage two-way communication with employees at regular meetings and through bulletin boards and the plant newspaper. When the effort was started, employees were suspicious and only questioned trite matters, such as coffee machine operation. But when management's sincerity became clear, the questioning became less guarded and more expansive. Searching questions about the company's long-range planning and other important policies were asked.

—Donnelly Mirrors, Inc., the major supplier of mirrors used in U.S. automobiles, organizes employees into work teams that tackle such questions as cost reduction, capital investment, compensation, and other matters. At meetings of the teams, discussion is free and open, and there seems to be a no-holds-barred attitude on criticism of any function of personalities in management.

—At Connecticut Mutual Life Insurance Company, a worker can get a free lunch by sitting at an executive's table in the cafeteria and taking part in a rap session where no questions are out of bounds.

—In an employee publication of American Airlines, one page is devoted to blunt questions and criticisms from employees. The attacks may range from the need for so many vice presidents to alleged management hypocrisies in dealing with the unions.

—In England, reports business writer Nancy Foy, the president of a large process company made significant changes in operations after he began sitting down with employees, leveling with them, and listening at length to their most devastating criticisms of management. Despite lack of cooperation from middle managers, the interchange led to significant changes in production and personnel policies, with the company going from a static, break-even level to a very profitable one.[2]

—In Scandinavia, as we saw earlier, employees exercise a profusion of rights in some companies which are among the world leaders in their fields. In West Germany, too, employees exercise far greater power than in the United States, and industry there has been notably successful. Although the Scandinavian and German cultures are different from the American, their experience cannot be dismissed out of hand.

Many organization officials, debating the case for giving employees freedom to speak out, visualize a scenario like the one in the movie *Barbarella*, where the main character, marooned in a wasteland, sees a host of beautiful automated dolls in the distance but, on drawing near, finds that their teeth are sharp and steely and that they emit shrill and piercing sounds. Unpleasant many of the voices of ungagged employees will probably be, but the examples reported above indicate no likelihood of the pandemonium that makes cooperation and efficiency impossible.

A classic formulation of the philosophy of the First Amendment was given decades ago by Supreme Court Justice Louis D. Brandeis. Although he was commenting on free speech in the political area, his observations would seem to be equally valid for the governance of corporations, public agencies, universities, and other organizations. Brandeis wrote:

> Those who won our independence . . . knew that order cannot be secured merely through fear of punishment for its infraction; that it is hazardous to discourage thought, hope and imagination; that fear breeds repression; that repression breeds hate; that hate menaces stable government; that the path of safety lies in the opportunity to discuss freely supposed grievances and proposed remedies . . . they eschewed silence coerced by law—the argument of force in its worst form.[3]

A similar view motivated Alexander Meiklejohn, the great philosopher of freedom of speech, to argue after World War II that neither the "clear and present danger" test nor any other notion of national security should be used to restrict freedom of speech except in the most extreme cases. The liberal view has also motivated various legal philosophers to argue in favor of generous First Amendment protection for so-called commercial speech, that is, corporate advertising, want ads, and other communications having to do with economic decision making between buyers and sellers. Franklyn S. Haiman, Martin Redish, and others feel that in the everyday lives of most people economic decisions are more challenging than political choices, and that to except them from the First Amendment protection perverts the philosophy of the Bill of Rights.[4] In 1974, the board of directors of the American Civil Liberties Union declared in favor of First Amendment protection for commercial as well as noncommercial speech.

Most businessmen would subscribe to this view. Apparently, however, many executives in business and government find the liberal view "unrealistic" when it comes to employee speech. In the name of discipline, they feel that free thinking about an organization's policies should be suppressed. In this respect, if no other, they are in league with radical left philosopher Herbert Marcuse, who argues that free speech cannot be justified when it becomes very distracting. Marcuse reaches the same conclusion (though by a different route) as did Nicolai Lenin, who said, "It is true that liberty is precious—so precious that it must be rationed."

What is the precise status of employee speech in U.S. organizations? Traditional rightlessness continues to be the rule. But exceptions to and inroads in the old law are being made. What most people believed to be an immutable pattern is proving quite changeable as judges, attorneys, and others place increased emphasis on other values.

INDUSTRY: THE GAG BEGINS TO LOOSEN

To understand what is going on, it is important to separate events in industry from those in government and public organizations.

In industry, the common law of nonfree speech—or, as a friend puts it, free nonspeech—applies most of the time. As discussed in chapters 1 and 2, since the management of a company or firm can fire an employee almost at will, it can effectively muzzle criticism or questioning of almost anything going on in the organization. The following three cases, decided in the early 1970s, each representing a major form of speech, affirm the traditional barriers:

1. When "Dick Echols," a guard in a power company, mentioned to a city official that management was wasting a lot of money on entertainment and "promotional expense," he got a twelve-day suspension. Because there was a union, Echols was able to protest his suspension by going to arbitration, but his efforts were a waste of time and money. Early in 1975 the arbitrator decided against him.[5]

2. In a case that caught the attention of numerous professional people, Louis V. McIntire brought suit in 1974 against the Du Pont Company, claiming that his discharge from the company's plastics plant in Orange, Texas, was unconstitutional. A chemical engineer, McIntire had worked for Du Pont from 1956 until 1972. During this period he was promoted several times and was paid respectable salaries. In 1972, however, his supervisors became acquainted with a novel he and his wife published in 1971 under the title, *Scientists and Engineers: The Professionals Who Are Not*. The novel was published by an unincorporated company set up by the author; about 2,000 copies were sold or distributed.

In the novel, a character named J. Marmaduke Glumm argues that technical employees should form a national federation to push legislation favoring its members. "It is a peculiar paradox," says Glumm, "that workingmen with little bargaining leverage have more actual job security than we do." Other characters in the novel inveigh against management for favoritism, screwing inventors out of bonuses they deserve for their discoveries, and taking unfair advantage of professionals in employment contracts. The fictional employer, Logan Chemical Company, is not too different from McIntire's real-life employer, Du Pont—the authors' criticisms are thinly veiled. It is not difficult to decide why some of his supervisors were displeased.

After his summary discharge, McIntire went to the Houston law firm of Combs & Archer, which took his case. In the Texas district court, he sued for $20 million. Late in 1974 the court threw out his claim that the First Amendment applied behind the corporate wall, that his constitutional right of free speech had been violated. However, other claims he made—that he had been blackballed among prospective employers after his discharge, that he had not been paid adequately for his inventions, that he had been denied due process—were still being litigated in 1977.

3. A chemical researcher wrote letters published by newspapers in which he charged the cosmetics industry, of

which his employer company was a member, with unconscionably high prices resulting from exorbitant advertising and promotion expenses. After he was sacked, he went to court alleging that his right to free speech had been infringed and that he was entitled to damages. The U.S. district court ruled that he did indeed have the right to free speech but not to a job in private industry. The company needed no reason at all for firing him so long as it did not violate employment laws concerning race and sex.[6]

Clearly the law says that there is no legal redress when unkind statements about a business employer or the industry are subject to harsh retaliation. But for those who hold the fortress against change, life is never simple. Even in industry, where the traditional line is hewed to most closely, cracks have appeared in the wall.

Companies with government contracts. In 1974 a federal court decided that a free-speaking employee has constitutional protection *if* his firm is deeply involved in work for the federal government. No precedent could be more dangerous from the standpoint of the authoritarian company. Unless this decision is forgotten or overruled, it could become the legal breach that the forces of change pour through. More and more companies do business off and on with the government—probably a majority of the 325,000 businesses making half a million dollars or more in annual profit. Many of them do not have substantial sales to the government, as the company to be described did, but can a logical line be drawn between the two groups? To do so would tax the ingenuity even of the courts. If a company with 80 percent sales to the government is subject to the new rule, why not a company with 50 percent of its sales to the government? And then why not a company with 35 percent government sales?

The case was decided by the U.S. District Court of Connecticut.[7] A skilled worker named Michael Holodnak, employed in Stratford, Connecticut by the Avco-Lycoming Division of Avco Corporation, wrote an article for a bi-weekly newsletter in New Haven that had a circulation of about 750 readers. In the article Holodnak accused Avco-Lycoming of sabotaging the grievance procedure (the company was unionized by the United Auto Workers); he also criticized the local union leadership for being passive. When the article was read by his bosses, they called him in, declared the article violated a rule of conduct for employees ("making false, vicious or malicious statements concerning . . . the employee's relationship" to the company), asked for his badge, and showed him to the door. Holodnak had worked in the plant for nine years.

First he went to arbitration. But the union attorney made only half-hearted attempts to defend him (in the opinion of the district court), and the arbitrator's decision went in favor of the company. Next Holodnak went to court.

The district court was impressed by the fact that Holodnak's article was "less vituperative and critical" of company practices than some of the union's own leaflets. It also felt he had not been given a fair shake in the grievance procedure. But most of all the court was impressed by Avco-Lycoming's relationship to the government. About 80 percent of production was military hardware—nose cones for missiles, helicopter engines, and so forth. While agreeing that the First Amendment does not apply to a private employer, the court noted that it did apply to public employees (it cited the *Pickering* case, to be described shortly). Therefore, workers at Avco-Lycoming were protected because of the "governmental presence" at the plant. The fact that Holodnak was speaking out on labor-management relations also helped his case. The district court ordered the company to make modest payments to Holodnak for wages lost and damages.

Special provisions in federal laws. Several federal statutes of the 1970s contain provisions forbidding businesses to penalize an employee who reports violations to the government agency in charge:

1. Coal Mine Safety Act, Section 110(b)—Management cannot discharge or discriminate against a miner who re-

ports alleged violations of the Act or dangers, who sues the company, or who testifies against it in court.

2. Occupational Safety and Health Act—Management may not discharge or discriminate against an employee who files a complaint about alleged violations of the Act. (If the employee requests anonymity, the Labor Department is required not to reveal his or her name to the employer.)

3. Water Pollution Control Act—Workers who report violations are protected in the same manner as under OSHA.

In addition, arbitrators and the courts have permitted employees to criticize employers for racial, sex, or age discrimination.[8]

Some observers fear that these first inroads against the nonfree speech principle will hit a dead end because of poor enforcement. The investigator at the Labor Department or other federal agency may choose to lengthen his coffee break instead of acting promptly on the complaint. Moreover, as we shall see in a later chapter, some authorities doubt that the statutes go far enough. If the employee gets reinstated, will he or she then get dumped or abused on trumped-up charges that the government will not want to fight? Without the possibility of greater gain, will employees decide in favor of discretion instead of valor? As the old saying goes, a closed mouth catches no flies.

These doubts may be valid. Even so, the statutes are important. For one thing, it appears that the provisions are being used, at least occasionally. For another, they set a standard to which wise men in management may wish to adhere. Perhaps most important, they set a precedent that is likely to take root and grow. Similar provisions may be cranked into other statutes. Judges sympathetic with employee rights may cite the provisions as evidence of the "tone" of the law. And the provisions dignify the action of reporting wrongdoing, making it evidence of "loyalty to the public interest" instead of "ratting on your employer."

Criticism of working conditions and labor relations. The National Labor Relations Act protects workers who speak out against work rules and other conditions. For instance, a group of research engineers protested having to fill out daily work logs and were fired for a spurious reason. When they haled the company before the National Labor Relations Board, they got their jobs back.[9] It did not matter that there was no union. (Judging from other decisions it did matter, though, that the protest was businesslike in tone and supported by a group of employees. The NLRB might not come to the aid of a single loudmouth who is fired.)

In another case, an employee meeting was being held on the question of unionization. After the plant manager finished blasting the idea, a known union supporter stood up and declared he had a question. When the manager ordered him to sit down, he wouldn't. The worker was then fired on grounds of insubordination. When he appealed to the NLRB, his discharge was ruled unlawful because speaking out is protected where employee efforts "to act in concert" are involved.[10] While there are earlier decisions that don't seem consistent with this one, it seems to convey the tone of current thinking in the government and the judiciary.

Criticism of union management. As Dean Lawrence E. Blades of the University of Iowa and other lawyers have noted, the courts have not protected from "abusive discharge" an employee who testifies against his employer in court. Since an employee is under oath then and supposedly trying to further the purposes of justice, this has been an especially galling rule for employee rights advocates. But there is an exception to it (other than the ones made in certain statutes, as noted above): A circuit court of appeals has held that an employee of a labor union could testify against the union at a legislative hearing.[11] Of course, a labor union is a not-for-profit organization, and therefore the case can be distinguished from those involving "ratters" in commercial firms, but there is reason to wonder if all judges will be impressed by that distinction. More than 20 million workers belong to labor unions. If employees of a union can testify under oath against it, then why not against the wrongdoing of their employers? If we go this far, then why not include other employees who are not unionized?

PUBLIC ORGANIZATIONS: THE FIRST AMENDMENT SHINES THROUGH

By themselves, the struggles to break the nonfree speech rule in industry may not seem important. Thus far, they have rescued relatively few employees, and as precedents the cases have little value if in the future the courts want to "quarantine" them. Since any future case that comes up is bound to be at least a little different in its facts, a judge simply has to "distinguish" it and apply the traditional rule. The battles won by attorneys in the Holodnak and other cases, and by the legislators of the safety and environmental laws, would then be of little consequence.

Such might be the probability but for another development: some decisive victories for employee rights in public organizations. About 14 million workers are classified as governmental. If their rights to speak out on controversial management policies are protected, for how long will it make sense to draw an iron curtain around the 60 million employees in business organizations, especially when (as we saw in Chapter 5) the government-business distinction is becoming blurred? Or around employees in other types of organizations that are neither governmental nor commercial, such as universities and arts organizations?

Before 1968 there were dissenting opinions, *obiter dicta*, law review articles, and other indications of an evolution in judicial thinking about the scope of the First Amendment. But it was in 1968 that the U.S. Supreme Court decided the case of an embattled high school teacher named Pickering, making the change official and indisputable.

Like many other teachers of English, history, math, the social sciences, and the arts, Pickering took a jaundiced view of the heavy emphasis on school athletics. But unlike most of his colleagues, Pickering was willing to stick his neck out. In a letter to the editor of a local newspaper, he lambasted the board of his school in Illinois. He claimed the board had built an athletic field out of bond funds, even though that was unauthorized. He charged the board with creating a "totalitarian atmosphere" and of lying to the public in order to gain support of high school athletics.

The letter was sarcastic. Some of the charges were true, some were untrue (according to the court's later findings). However, Pickering did not try to shoot down particular officials with whom he worked. What is more, he was not the one who stirred up the argument; the school board's policy had been debated already in the town. These facts were to become important.

Pickering was fired. Seeking reinstatement, he went to the Illinois courts and lost. Then he went to the U.S. Supreme Court and won.[12] "On such a question free and open debate is vital to informed decision making by the electorate," the Supreme Court stated, and teachers should not be "compelled to relinquish the First Amendment rights they would otherwise enjoy as citizens to comment on matters of public interest." The Supreme Court emphasized that Pickering's blast did not maim individuals with whom he worked, thus upsetting morale and the normal operations of his department.

The *Pickering* decision and the mood it symbolized have caused a chain reaction in the judiciary. For example:

—A Chicago policeman was fired for derogatory comments about the city's police department. After waiting in vain for some response by his superiors to his claim that other policemen were taking stolen property they recovered in their duties, he suggested on a television news program that his bosses were covering up. In 1970 a federal court ordered him reinstated and also called unconstitutional a police force rule prohibiting derogatory comments about the organization.[13]

—In 1971 an elementary school teacher was given First Amendment protection for criticizing matters closer to home than Pickering had. She had publicly voiced concern about the hazard of an open incinerator on the school playground; in addition, she had helped her students draft a letter to the school cafeteria requesting that it serve raw as well as cooked carrots. Though she had taught for more than twenty-five years, her contract was not renewed. Relying on the *Pickering* decision but broadening its application, the circuit court reasoned: "When a School Board acts, as it did here, to punish a teacher who seeks to protect the health and safety of herself and her pupils, the resulting intimidation can only cause a severe chilling, if not freezing, effect on the free discussion of more controversial subjects."[14]

—In a 1973 case, a nurse in a psychiatric hospital won reinstatement after she was fired because of a news article in which the reporter quoted her criticisms of patient care and medical staff behavior at the hospital. The federal court held that she "was engaging in precisely the sort of free and vigorous expression that the First Amendment was designed to protect," even though her criticisms may have caused some anxiety on the staff.[15]

—A fireman named Dendor said the village fire marshal did not know how to manage the fire department and would cause disaster. For thus arousing his superiors' dander, Dendor got sacked. When he went to court, management defended its actions on the ground that Dendor was undermining the discipline, morale, and efficiency of the fire department by his outspokenness. But management could not prove actual damage to the force, nor could it prove that Dendor himself was "unfit for public service." Therefore the circuit court in 1973 decided in Dendor's favor.[16]

These cases, while not the whole story, demonstrate how, following 1968, the courts made the umbrella of the *Pickering* case larger. That is significant because it shows that *Pickering* was no mere aberration but a decision that other judges want to respond to. One of the few exceptions is a decision by the state supreme court of Alaska, which apparently did *not* feel comfortable with the *Pickering* decision. In a case similar to *Pickering,* it upheld a school board for lowering the boom on an outspoken teacher. It found a way to distinguish its case from the one the U.S. Supreme Court had decided. But that was in 1969, and efforts to buck the *Pickering* trend have not been notable since then.[17]

Because their attorneys frequently advise employers to settle out of court, some potentially interesting cases have never been tried. Joan T. Lentczner was publications adviser at Yorktown High School in Indiana. She made the mistake, in the principal's view, of approving publication of a series of articles on sex in the student newspaper. The principal fired her. On the ground that her constitutional rights had been infringed, in 1974 she sued the school for reinstatement and for punitive damages of $33,000. The Indiana Civil Liberties Union and several professional groups gave her financial support; the media helped her; and of course her lawyer was able to cite cases with precedential value. Her arguments were strong enough to make the school decide to settle out of court.

If the *Pickering* philosophy has become so strong, why has it been necessary for Senators Kennedy, Proxmire, and others to come to the rescue of beleaguered whistle-blowers in Washington agencies (as we saw in Chapter 5)?

One reason is that the common law (that is, judge-made law) takes root one case at a time; it does not have immediate, sweeping, well-defined application as a statute does. Therefore uncertainty exists as to whether the *Pickering* rule applies across the board, to agencies of the executive arm of government as well as to city schools, hospitals, fire departments, and the other subjects of court decisions since 1968. A second reason is that an ancient tradition with centuries of momentum cannot, as the saying goes, stop on a dime. Managers are so used to stamping out dissidence among employees that it is hard for them to believe the law says no. Think how long after 1954 it took for the Supreme Court's historic decision on school segregation, *Brown* v. *Board of Education,* to be implemented.

But probably the most important reason that whistle-blowers require the assistance of legislators is the risk, difficulty, and expense of taking an employer to court. A case in point involves three engineers in San Francisco. When the Bay Area Rapid Transit (BART) system was planned, several years ago, these men found fault with it. They said the automatic controls planned would be unsafe, and passed their criticisms on to a member of the board of BART. The board member mentioned the criticisms at a public meeting. The three engineers were fired as trouble makers. The California Society of Professional Engineers, of which they were members, investigated the case and found they had "acted in the interest of the public welfare." It gave them moral support in their efforts to seek redress from BART, but it declined to join in their legal suit for damages.

Left on their own, the engineers settled the case out of court. Presumably they received less compensation than they would have from a judge, if they had won the case, but this expectation was more than offset by the great expense of litigation. As a result, a court ruling was never made which might have proved to be of enormous value to other engineers and scientists who might be tempted to blow the whistle on wrongdoing in their organizations. Not surprisingly, the employee rights movement has been advancing more slowly and less certainly than it might have in a sector that many observers regard as a very promising one for action.

DRAWING THE LINE

In our political and social lives, freedom of speech and press are qualified only a little. We do not have the right to yell "Fire!" in a crowded movie theater. We are not entitled to slander our neighbor. In times of national emergency we are not free to promulgate information that may give comfort to the enemy. A few other qualifications exist.

But in organizational life, freedom of speech must be qualified a great deal more. We must draw rigorous limits or run the risk of making it needlessly difficult to manage, thus jeopardizing the capacity of organizations to function effectively. What kinds of speech should *not* be protected in business, governmental, and other organizations? I phrase the question in this manner on purpose, for it is better to state negative injunctions, instead of positive ones, in order to provide maximum generality for free speech.

First, no employee should have a right to divulge information about legal and ethical plans, practices, operations, inventions, and other matters that the organization must keep confidential in order to do its job in an efficient manner. A few years ago the president of Swarthmore College was disturbed by the demands zealous government officials were making on faculty, staff, and students. He warned the Swarthmore community that "those who divulge confidential information not demanded by law or college policy risk dismissal."

Second, no employee should have a right to make personal accusations or slurs which are irrelevant to questions about policies and actions that seem illegal or irresponsible. A union official shouted at her supervisor, "You are a goddam cheap Jew!" When she was fired, she took the case to arbitration; the arbitrator refused to reinstate her.[18] This decision was correct. In another case, the arbitrator refused to reinstate a worker who, when warned by a guard against taking a radio out of the plant, called the guard a pig and other choice epithets.[19] This decision, too, was correct. In cases of this sort, the verbal abuse has no value for the organization or the public.

Third, no employee should be entitled to disrupt an organization or hurt its morale by making speeches and accusations that do not reflect a conviction that wrong is being done. The employee who talks about "the crooks who run this place," or who gives newspapers phony stories about the morals or misbehavior of top executives—these people deserve no protection. (However, it is not necessary that all of an employee's claims be true, if they seem to have been made in good faith. For example, as the Supreme Court noted, not all of Pickering's accusations could be supported by the evidence.)

Fourth, no employee should be entitled to rail against the competence of a supervisor or senior manager to make everyday work decisions that have nothing to do with the legality, morality, or responsibility of management actions. This is the most difficult criterion. The distinction between internal squabbles and workaday operations, on the one hand, and an organization's public posture and morality, on the other, is not always easy to make. Yet it must be made as intelligently as possible. If it is not made, either employee rights will run wild, or they will be so hedged as to be meaningless. The former would happen if, let us say, tirades against management's judgment in cost cutting were protected. What manager could expect to get a day's work out if he was forced to heed this sort of carping?

In addition to these four rules, no employee is entitled to object to discharge, transfer, or demotion, no matter what he has said about the organization or how he has said it, if management can demonstrate that unsatisfactory performance or violation of a code of conduct was the reason for its action. This requirement is crucial. If it is not observed, then all an employee need do to keep his job is start raising questions about management wrongdoing and shout "Foul!" when he gets fired for doing lousy work.

How can management prove that performance, not exercise of the First Amendment, dictated its action? One good answer is a supervisor's log showing specific incidents of failure or so-so performance. Such an approach has been in use in some companies for many years, simply to improve the quality of supervision. It has also been a tool of managers in making performance appraisals of subordinates.

Recently some authorities have urged written documentation as a defense in age-discrimination suits by employees. By keeping records showing examples of unsatisfactory performance, and perhaps of a supervisor's talk with the employee about it, management can fend off legal claims by employees who allege they were let go for reasons of age rather than inability to perform. If a log can work for purposes like these, it should serve the need of an honest manager in a free speech case.

THE GROWING TENSION

The movement toward free speech in organizations was not
planned. It just happened to start as it did. The companies
that experimented with two-way communication were
thinking in terms of "job enrichment," "participative management," or other philosophies; they did not propose to
carry the torch of a new crusade. The federal legislators who
have tried to protect the free-speaking employees of government agencies appear to have been motivated by a desire to obtain evidence about inept and misguided agency
leadership; they did not see themselves in the role of
modern-day Thomas Paines. Nor did the judges who decided the *Pickering* line of cases work from a plan of revolution; the cases were brought to them because of events over
which they had no control. As for Holodnak, Pickering, Rafferty, Dendor, and the other outspoken employees who
went to court, they were fighting partly out of anger and
partly to save their skins.

Now that the starting gate has opened and the corporate,
legislative, and legal horses are off, however, all sorts of
tensions are being created. How they will be resolved, and
how fast, is a question no one can answer now, but it seems
sure that historic events are under way. We couldn't return,
even if we tried, to the obliviousness and indifference to
employee speech that existed before the late 1960s.

For employees, there is the tension created by the example of the Holodnaks and the Pickerings. "If they did it, why
shouldn't I?" is a question that many more people in industry and government are going to be asking themselves. Fortunately for most of them, a court fight will not be necessary.

For members of top management there will be tension,
too. There will be not only the uneasiness of having to field
difficult questions and learn unpleasant things, but there
will also be a need to redefine their own roles. Albert Z.
Carr described a conversation he had with a successful
executive of a large corporation. In a confidential moment,

the executive said he had become unhappy about the irresponsible behavior he saw going on in parts of management. But what were his options? If he started speaking out, he would be branded a dissident and his career would be jeopardized. If he stayed silent, he would lose respect for himself. If he resigned and went to another company, he would probably succeed in exchanging one set of moral misgivings for another. He told Carr how he envied his associates whose consciences had not developed beyond the Neanderthal stage and who could accept things as they were. He wondered if he should try to train himself in indifference. Carr added:

> Perhaps he made this effort and succeeded in it, for he remained with the company and forged ahead. He may even have fancied that he had killed his conscience—as the narrator in Mark Twain's symbolic story did when he gradually reached the point where he could blithely murder the tramps who came to his door asking for handouts.
>
> But conscience is never killed; when ignored, it merely goes underground, where it manufactures the toxins of suppressed guilt, often with serious psychological and physical consequences.[20]

Now that speaking out has won some form of legal respectability, more top executives will feel conflicts like the one described, and it will not be so easy to become indifferent.

For legislators and judges there will be great tensions. Current inconsistencies in the law are especially difficult to live with. Employees of a company selling 80 percent of its products to the government have a right to free speech, but not the employees of companies doing little business with the government. An employee who reports violations of the Coal Mine Safety, Water Pollution Control, or Occupational Safety and Health Acts is protected, but not workers who blow the whistle on other important violations, such as illegal political payoffs, distortion of information about product safety, and questionable financial deals. A worker is protected when testifying against his union but not when testifying against his company (at least, in most states). An employee of a hospital has a right to speak out about poor practices, but an employee of a drug firm or medical supply company who does so can be crucified. An employee of a school system has a right to criticize irresponsible actions of the school board, but an employee of a textbook publisher who criticized the board of directors for irresponsible policies could be sacked immediately.

Inconsistencies like these are going to disturb legislators and judges until rights are either pruned back or expanded. Since pruning back appears contrary to the tide of opinion, expansion seems to be the logical solution.

For the public, too, there will be tensions. As organizations lose their ability to control the news about them, stockholders, creditors, suppliers, and friends of employees will find themselves pondering conflicting facts and viewpoints. The business pages of newspapers, traditionally as lively as a Soviet news release, will become more controversial, more like those pages reporting on city hall, the statehouse, and the White House. Will society consider this a cost or a benefit? In rendering its opinion on an employee speech case in 1973, the California Supreme Court stated:

> Disharmony and friction are the healthy but natural results of a society which cherishes the right to speak freely on a subject and the resultant by-products should never prevent an individual from speaking or cause that individual to be penalized for such speech.[21]

About a year later, U.S. Supreme Court Justice Lewis F. Powell wrote for the Court:

> Under the First Amendment there is no such thing as a false idea. However pernicious an opinion may seem, we depend for its correction not on the consciences of judges and juries but on the competition of other ideas.[22]

NOTES

1. John J. O'Connor, *New York Times*, December 6, 1973.
2. Nancy Foy, "Pathways to Participation," *Management Today*, January 1974, p. 95.
3. *Whitney* v. *California*, 47 S. Ct. 641, 648.
4. See Franklyn S. Haiman, "How Much of Our Speech Is Free?" *Civil Liberties Review*, Winter 1975, pp. 111–137.
5. *Employee Relations in Action* (New York, Man & Manager), March 1975. All names that appear in this publication are fictional.
6. *Employee Relations in Action*, December 1971.
7. *Holodnak* v. *Avco Corporation, Avco-Lycoming Division, et al.*, Civil Action No. B-15 (1974), U.S. District Court, Connecticut.
8. *White Collar Management* (New York, Man & Manager), May 1, 1974.
9. *White Collar Management*, February 1, 1973.
10. *Prescott Industrial Products Co.*, an NLRB case reported in *Labor Law Journal*, September 1973, p. 642.
11. *Petermann* v. *International Brotherhood of Teamsters*, 344 P. 2d 25 (1959).
12. *Pickering* v. *Board of Education*, 391 U.S. 563 (1968).
13. *Muller* v. *Conlisk*, 429 F. 2d 901 (1970).
14. *Downs* v. *Conway School District*, 328 F. Supp. 338 (1971).
15. *Rafferty* v. *Philadelphia Psychiatric Center*, 356 F. Supp. 500 (1973).
16. *Dendor* v. *Board of Fire and Police Commissioners*, 297 N.E. 2d 316 (1973).
17. *Watts* v. *Seward School Board*, 454 P. 2d 732 (1969). Three other cases taking an anti-Pickering posture are *Fisher* v. *Walker*, 464 F. 2d 1147 (1972), *Murphy* v. *Facendia*, 307 F. Supp. 353 (1969), and *Meehan* v. *Macy*, 392 F. 2d 822 (1968).
18. *Employee Relations in Action*, July 1975.
19. *Protection Management* (New York, Man & Manager), no. 2009 (1975), p. 1.
20. Albert Z. Carr, "Can An Executive Afford a Conscience?" *Harvard Business Review*, July-August 1960, p. 60.
21. *Adcock* v. *Board of Education*, 513 P. 2d 900 (1973), quoted in Kenneth D. Walters, "Your Employees' Right to Blow the Whistle," *Harvard Business Review*, July-August 1975, p. 31.
22. See Anthony Lewis, "Free Speech: Never Total, Once Again Expanding," *New York Times*, February 8, 1976.

7

MORE SCOPE
FOR
CONSCIENCE
AND CHOICE

"I was profoundly impressed as a young man by the example of our company's founder, Solomon Agoos," the export manager of Allied Kid Company once said. "His behavior in the financial crisis of 1920, when the market for leather goods broke, was exemplary. All of his employees appreciated the level at which he wanted the business conducted. For example, no one would think of yielding to pressure from even the largest foreign customer for false invoices, which would enable the customer to evade customs duties."[1]

At a time when newspapers are constantly reporting cases of misconduct in business and government, Solomon Agoos's example may seem anomalous. Actually it is not. Thousands of organizations maintain high ethical standards, and thousands of others make a valiant effort to do so. If this were not true, an employee bill of rights would be pointless—trying to change the situation would be like trying to force a glacier to retreat.

Yet in every organization, even the most exemplary, there is a problem. The devil may be out of sight but he is never far away. Let the good intentions falter or become beclouded just for an instant, and the temptation triumphs. One unhappy result is the unethical or immoral directive issued to a subordinate who does not want to comply but knows that refusal will lead to dismissal or other forms of retaliation. Even though such orders might account for only a tiny percentage of a corporation's or agency's work orders, they are significant. Like a drop of misplaced color on a painting, they have an effect out of proportion to their statistical amount. They become the subject of fast-spreading gossip. And for the unhappy subordinate who must comply or quit, the ethical conflict may turn into an infectious disease of mind and spirit.

In every business, civic, and government organization there should be freedom to refuse to carry out an unethical directive without threat of punishment. Such a right would reward and enhance personal integrity besides providing a valuable source of feedback and control for top management. Many organization leaders know that a vexing tendency in large organizations is for an employee mistakenly to assume that the unethical conduct of a supervisor is condoned by senior managers. The employee thinks cynically, "All the brass are in cohoots." When subordinates refuse to go along with such a supervisor, thus bringing his behavior to the attention of superiors, top management has an opportunity to express its disapproval and clarify policy for the whole organization.

ETHICAL TENTERHOOKS

The most numerous and most important ethical decisions confronting an employee are not those of out-and-out illegality but those at the fringes of the law. In these cases the unhappy subordinate has no recourse. He could not get help from the law if he tried. He could not even get a newspaper reporter to write up the story. Yet his sense of morality and perhaps his religious convictions are violated.

What happens if the employee says to the boss, "Hold it. This act isn't right"? An analogy of the likely result comes from novelist Elia Kazan. While he snorkeled in the Pacific, Kazan observed herds of fish grazing. They moved slowly along the bottom, heads down, feeding. Barracuda could be seen hovering a short distance away. For a long time there might be no kill. But then one of the fish in the herd would start wobbling—an injured fin, perhaps, or some other difficulty. As if by some common signal, the rest slowly would move away from the faltering fish. After it was separated, in one terrible second the barracuda would attack, seize it in its jaws, and with a shake, snap, and crunch, dispose of it. In the meantime the rest of the herd would go on grazing a little way off, heads down—"business as usual."

In a despotic organization the violence is only economic and emotional, of course, but after the dissident employee is "destroyed"—or his or her job is destroyed, in the case of an agency subject to Civil Service rules precluding outright dismissal—there is a tendency for the others to return to business as usual. People keep their heads down.

Judging from many reports, the following examples are not unusual:

—Shirley Zinman, a secretary who refused to tape telephone conversations with clients of her firm, without their knowledge, was able to qualify for unemployment compensation when she resigned her job, but the necessity of her resigning was not questioned.[2]

—Judging from testimony given the U.S. Senate's Health Subcommittee of the Labor and Public Welfare Committee, in August 1974, some sections of the Food and Drug Administration expected researchers to report only in a favorable way on certain drugs about to go on the market. (Usually these were drugs that top officials approved after receiving at least some evidence of their suitability and safety.) When eleven physicians and researchers refused to confirm that these drugs were safe, they were harassed and intimidated. About half of them were transferred to jobs for which they were ill suited, an obvious attempt to get them to resign. For instance, Dr. Carol Kennedy, a psychiatrist, recommended against a drug which was to be sold to children. In an obvious attempt to goad her to resign, her superiors transferred her to the dental-surgical section to study soft contact lenses.

—A factory was making plans for expansion. The new general manager went over the details with the facilities engineer, an older man who was a few years away from comfortable retirement—if he kept his pension. The general manager, who wanted to make a good profit showing, insisted that the engineer specify footings and structural steel specifications that were below the standards of good practice. When the engineer balked, he was told to choose between doing as he was told and losing his job.

—A corporate controller drew up a profit-and-loss statement for the year which showed a loss. The company was trying to get an important loan from a bank. The executive vice-president told the controller to revise the figures so that a profit showed on the bottom line. The controller refused. He was fired on the spot.[3]

—In a service organization, a woman in the administrative department caught the eye of a senior male manager. When she refused his sexual advances, she was dismissed on the pretext of a "reorganization." The senior manager stayed on.[4]

With the stimulation only of a cocktail and a confidential atmosphere, knowledgeable people in business and government can supply endless examples of this sort. Price rigging, discriminatory treatment, influence peddling, veiled threats, cheating, dishonest reports, "call girls"—the list goes on and on. Usually the acts are a product of several kinds of stress, organizational and personal. Except in the organization that, to use Christopher Stone's phrase, is "born crooked," there is likely to be more sympathy with the victimized employee than with the offending superior.

In a survey which drew extensive answers from 3,453 managers, I found that a strong majority took the side of an accountant who (in a case described to respondents) refused to doctor the figures to change a loss into a profit.[5] More than nine-tenths of managers at all levels felt that such a person *should* be reinstated, if fired; three-fourths of them believed that their organization *would* reinstate the employee if the case came to light. (Many more respondents would go along with firing an employee who blabbered about such an incident to an important outsider, causing harm to the organization. Only about two-fifths said they would reinstate the employee in that case.)

In another questionnaire survey that I sent out early in 1977, a strong majority of business executives again took the side of the employee in cases where a person was fired for refusing to obey unethical directives. A great many managers expressed willingness to "rock the boat," if necessary, to get the victim back in the job.

What right should an employee have in cases of this sort? In proposing an answer, two practical considerations should be kept in mind.

First, the employee often assumes that ethics and morality are being violated when they are not. Once the boss's side is presented sympathetically, the case ceases to be open-and-shut. In fact, often the employee will be able to gain little support for his viewpoint.

Second, it may be very important to do the disputed act quickly, if it is to be done at all. The organization cannot wait for the case to be heard and resolved. Assuming that employees' perceptions of the devil are often distorted, an organization could be brought to its knees if the bosses' decisions were held up. Failing to meet a deadline often means failure to avert disaster or to seize a golden opportunity.

What right would be appropriate then? The employee should be able to refuse to carry out the order without losing his job or prospects for promotion, if his objection is sincere and reasonable. On the other hand, the boss should immediately be free to ask someone else to do the job. Afterwards, if the boss wants to challenge the employee for being obstructive, he can request a hearing on the incident. Or he can penalize the employee and let the employee request the hearing.

In one case, an assistant refused to doctor a press release describing tests on the safety of a product; he felt the word changes wanted by the boss created a false and misleading impression. Because the timing was urgent, the boss turned immediately to someone else and said, "Okay, you do it." The second person did as requested. Afterwards there continued to be differences of opinion in the department as to whether the doctoring was ethical.

Much to his credit, the manager in this case did not penalize the first assistant when the time came for annual pay increases. "I wouldn't have had him on my staff if I didn't think he was good. I gave him increases before and intend to do so again, if he keeps up the good work."

OUTSIDE ACTIVITIES OF INNER-DIRECTED PEOPLE

Many organizations prohibit their employees from engaging in social causes, political groups, and other outside activities of their choice because a senior official frowns on such associations. Traditionally employers have been able to control as many outside activities of employees as they knew about. Lawrence Stessin quotes the rules of a New York carriage shop in force in 1878. "It is expected that each employee shall participate in the activities of the church and contribute liberally to the Lord's work," states one of the rules. Another rule says: "All employees are expected to be in bed by 10:00 P.M. Except: Each male employee may be given one evening a week for courting purposes. . . ."

Few employers, if any, make such extreme edicts today, but other requirements they try to impose are distasteful to many employees (including managers) and offensive to much of the public. For instance, William W. Wheeler, in the interview described earlier, made it clear he did not want to see any employee of Phillips Petroleum at a competitor's gas station. Presumably the chief executive would have turned against the deviant even if "the rest of the pack" didn't.

There is growing distaste for this sort of stricture on the outside activities of an employee. In Arizona, California, and Florida it is unlawful for an employer to direct employees to purchase or not to purchase goods from certain suppliers. Again, in the arbitration case of *Paul Swanson*, the arbitrator ruled that working in the service department of a Ford Motor Company agency does not mean that the employee has to "like" the cars being serviced. The employee had gone out and bought a Rambler; because of this he was discharged. The arbitrator ordered the man back to the job, saying that so long as his work was satisfactory and he did not disparage the employer's product in such a way as to hurt the business, his feelings about an auto for his own use were his own affair.[6] Had there not been a supportive union and an arbitration process, however, it is doubtful the employee could have been reinstated.

Perhaps the most controversial type of constraint is political. If a company, public agency, educational institution, union, or other organization is controlled by managers who have strong feelings about a particular political cause, the term of employment may be brief for the worker who espouses the other side. Reacting to information that some top executives of banks had been urging employees to contribute to certain political causes, U.S. Senator William Proxmire stated in 1974:

> When the president of a bank sends out a letter to his employees "suggesting" an appropriate contribution to a political fund controlled by the bank, I wonder how many employees really consider the contribution to be voluntary? Regardless of what the top officials of the bank may claim, an employee cannot help but think his chances of promotion within the bank depend upon whether he makes the political contribution.

One of the banks Proxmire may have been referring to was Security National. According to the U.S. Department of Justice, which gained the information from several of the bank's executives, high-level employees who were up for promotion were required to donate up to $2,000 of their raises to a secret political fund maintained by top officials of Security National.[7] No donation, no move forward.

The press has described the same sort of pressure in government agencies. For example, in 1973 the *Boston Globe* reported that some city employees had been instructed to work on "company time" as well as after hours for certain candidates favored by Mayor Kevin White. The instructions came in the form of polite requests for volunteers from the mayor's assistants, but the aggrieved employees made it clear the action was comparable to an Army sergeant's picking of "volunteers." Fearing retribution if their protests were known, they remained anonymous in the *Globe*'s report.

In another publicized case, Bethlehem Steel Company in 1964 fired Philip B. Woodroofe, its supervisor of municipal services, for going to work for the Community Civic League in Bethlehem, Pennsylvania. This league sought to improve racial relations and was supported by both black and white community leaders. Reportedly, Woodroofe was told to get out of the League; he refused. A few days later he was told "you're through." He was given to understand that it would not be enough if his wife took over his responsibilities in the League; neither of them could be involved. In the ensuing uproar, the company protested that it had fired Woodroofe because his involvement in the League would be taken "as an expression of the official position of the company." "I am on the Red Cross Board," Woodroofe said. "I don't speak for the company there."[8]

An ironic aspect of such cases is that they occur in the organization that proclaims lofty ideals of individualism as well as in the organization that doesn't. What mayor, governor, or chairman of a federal agency has not spoken eloquently in favor of individualism, especially political individualism? Corporate heads, too, wave the flag. The chief executive officer of Bethlehem Steel, some time before the Woodroofe incident, had addressed the local Chamber of Commerce and emphasized that "our employees are encouraged to participate as fully as they can in the life of the community, as citizens, irrespective of their status with the company."

A number of states have statutes making it unlawful for an employer to prevent employees from engaging in certain political activities; these states include Arizona, California, Massachusetts, Minnesota, Missouri, and Wisconsin. As we shall see later, however, the legal remedy is weak for an employee who gets fired and seeks the protection of the law. The possible penalties favor the employer. As for the common law, the courts have ruled that the Bill of Rights applies to interference by the states with a citizen's political activities, not to constraints by his business employer.[9]

How free should employees be to engage in outside activities of their own choosing? So long as their activities do not cause palpable harm to the organization, they should be free to buy whatever products and services they wish from whatever source; they should be free to work for political, community, and social causes of their own choice; they should be free to engage in whatever other outside activities satisfy them. Job security and advancement should not be denied them for any of these choices, no matter how differently the boss or employer feels about the outside activity.

The employer organization, too, has important rights to protect. What kinds of outside activity should *not* be privileged because of the palpable harm they may do to the firm or agency? Here are some examples:

—In arbitration cases, arbitrators frequently have upheld disciplinary action against employees who have taken on outside jobs—"moonlighting"—that place them in competition with their employers.

—Several years ago McGraw-Hill Book Company fired some young women activists. One of them accused the company of maintaining a "repressive atmosphere." Edward Booher, the chief executive, countered that the young woman was discharged not because of her activities per se but because of their effect on her work. "She made a real nuisance of herself with her peer group, plus the fact that her many outside activities—women's lib and what have you—began to interfere with the quality of her work." Assuming he was right, this is a legitimate reason for discharge.

—An employee called in to report he was sick. Later in the day his foreman happened to meet him outside a tavern. The foreman said he'd be interested in the real reason the employee didn't show up for work. (The employee had been drunk all day, it turned out.) The worker attacked the foreman. The arbitrator allowed a six-month suspension of the worker.[10]

—A veteran meter tester in the employ of Tri-State Gas and Electric Company went to the homes of company customers, after working hours, and preached to them the doctrines of Jehovah's Witnesses. Various customers complained to the company; some said the employee had become angry when asked to leave the home. They said they would not have let him come in but for his being a Tri-State meter tester, and demanded that management stop his visits. The man was told to stop; he said he wouldn't. The company fired him.[11]

It is not possible to draw a clear line between what is permissible and what is not. There is a large gray area where account must be taken of the personalities involved, the community mood, the particular position of the employer organization, and other considerations.

One case that fell into such a gray area involved two energetic employees who set up a bar with go-go girls near the employer's plant. Calling them in, the vice-president said, "You know we are tolerant of moonlighting around here, but this isn't the kind of thing our employees should be doing. We are the biggest company in the community and we want to keep on good terms with all our neighbors." The two entrepreneurs refused to stop, claiming that the bar was legitimate, a popular place to go, and that their work in the company was not affected. They were fired. The arbitrator gave them back their jobs.[12] The decision is debatable. Cases similar *in principle* might be decided the other way by competent arbitrators, depending on the individual coloration of the situation.

When management claims an outside activity is harming on-the-job performance, will its claims be rejected by union officials and arbitrators? Not if it has evidence in the file about failures at work. As emphasized earlier, it is important for senior managers to be able to point to specific notes describing inadequate or deteriorating performance. In the absence of such data, arbitrators, ombudspeople, and others may well shrug their shoulders at the most insistent claims of an angry boss.

THE METHOD IS THE MESSAGE

What astonishes many observers about reports of ethical misconduct and oppression in management is that the wrongdoers often are friendly, likable, capable, and even idealistic people. They are not con men or toughs. How is it possible for managers and officials like these to make such mistakes?

One answer comes from Duncan E. Littlefair. Evil may not be easy to recognize, Littlefair points out.[13] In melodramas and Westerns, wickedness is easy enough to see. But in real life evil may be friendly, open, and attractive.

Many of the culprits in cases like those we have reviewed may have acted out of sincere conviction that the goals justified the methods or out of loyalty to associates who desired the action taken. This seems to have been the pattern even in some cases of extreme wrongdoing. In the notorious Equity Funding Life Insurance case, for instance, more than a hundred people seem to have known what was going on, but many felt it would be disloyal to "rat" on friends and associates. Again, some business leaders who connived in the early 1970s to make illegal political payments or to bribe officials of foreign governments first became involved out of a belief that they were protecting the jobs and interests of employees in their organizations.

Americans, especially American managers, place enormous value on "getting results." What is accomplished tends to win more plaudits than how the result was obtained, and goals receive more attention than methods. From the standpoint of justice and morality it should be the other way around. Looking back on his diplomatic service in the Soviet Union during World War II, George F. Kennan reflects:

> It was primarily against people's methods rather than against their objectives that [my] indignation mounted. . . . Objectives were normally vainglorious, unreal, extravagant, even pathetic—little likely to be realized, scarcely to be taken seriously. People had to have them, or to believe they had them. It was part of their weakness as human beings. But methods were another matter. These were real. It was out of their immediate effects that the quality of life was really molded. In war as in peace I found myself concerned less with what people thought they were striving for than with the manner in which they strove for it.[14]

While Kennan's criticisms of objectives surely are too strong for most American organizations, the rest of his observation could stand in almost any setting. Whether in a corporation, a public agency, or a professional firm, the quality of life depends more on the *way* work is done than on the conventional indicators of management success, such as quantity of output, financial achievements, or long-range goals.

NOTES

1. Raymond C. Baumhart, "How Ethical Are Businessmen?" *Harvard Business Review*, July-August 1961, p. 158.
2. 8 Pa. Comm. Ct. Reports 649, 304 A. 2d 380 (1973). The case is described in more detail in Chapter 1.
3. Baumhart, pp. 164–165.
4. In at least one case where the object of a male superior's attentions was a member of the union, a female employee was reinstated after complaining to the union. See *Monge* v. *Beebe Rubber Company*, 316 A. 2d 549, 550 (1974).
5. David W. Ewing, "Who Wants Employee Rights?" *Harvard Business Review*, November-December 1971, p. 32.
6. *Paul Swanson*, 61-2 ARB 8303, 1961 (CCH).
7. *New York Times*, May 30, 1974.
8. "Bethlehem Steel Company and the Woodroofe Incident," Intercollegiate Clearing House case No. 14H20, Boston, Mass. 02163.
9. See "Discrimination: Can an Employee Be Fired for Belonging to a 'Hate' Group?" *The Businessman and the Law* (New York, N.Y., Man & Manager) July 1, 1974, reporting on an employee fired for belonging to the Klu Klux Klan.
10. *Sundstrand Corp.*, 66-1 ARB 8308 (CCH). Depending on individual circumstances, other arbitration cases involving fighting have been decided in favor of the employee.
11. "Tri-State Gas and Electric Company: The Difficult Case of Jeffrey Porter," in Benjamin M. Selekman, Stephen H. Fuller, Thomas Kennedy, and John Baitsell, *Problems in Labor Relations* (New York: McGraw-Hill Book Company, 1964), pp. 155–161.
12. *Employee Relations in Action*, January 1968, no. 385.
13. Duncan E. Littlefair, *Sin Comes of Age* (Philadelphia: Westminster Press, 1975), pp. 28–32.
14. George F. Kennan, *Memoirs, 1925–1950* (Boston: Little, Brown and Company, 1967), p. 199.

8

PRIVACY
VS.
INTRUSION:
DARKNESS AT NOON?

When employees talk candidly about their jobs in business and public organizations, they often criticize management for snooping and bureaucratic harassment. This is one of the themes running through Studs Terkel's book *Working.*[1] Of course, management doesn't see its activity this way. To management, detection practices are part of an effort to control employee output and assure productivity. Most supervisors, middle managers, and other executives share Samuel Johnson's opinion—they fear that where there is mystery, roguery is not far off.

Traditionally, the law has favored employer attitudes of "the less employee privacy, the better." Thus, the personnel records of employees are not confidential. Authorities agree that the constitutional concept of a right to privacy has had little influence on personnel relations. Even when an employer misuses personal information about an employee and the employee is fortunate enough to find out, the way to a remedy can be very difficult. "Claims by an employee who has been injured by misuse of his personal information may fall between the effective privacy and defamation causes of action," states Mordechai Mironi, an attorney and researcher at the University of Minnesota.[2]

An employee's privacy is invaded twice in organizations

that exercise the full freedom given them by the traditional
law. First, it is invaded when the employer collects data
about the worker. Exhaustive questionnaires about the person's life and habits, psychological tests, and electronic
tests—even their enthusiastic supporters in personnel departments admit that they raise a legitimate question of unfair invasion. But they insist that the benefit to management
and society outweighs the invasion. Second, the employee's
privacy is invaded when the information collected is put to
use. Managers make decisions on the basis of information
the employee may not know about, including hearsay comments and off-the-cuff opinions gleaned from quick interviews. The organization uses the same information to answer inquiries from social workers, credit bureaus, union
officials, insurance companies, lawyers, government agencies, and other sources.

"What is common to all these episodes," writes Mironi,
"is that personal information initially revealed by a job
seeker in order to get a job, or collected by an employer
throughout and as part of the employment relationship, is
released for a purpose that has nothing to do with the job
and perhaps is against the employee's interest."[3] Thus a
whole block of an employee's private life may bob to the
surface at an unexpected place downstream, for other view-
ers along the bank to see. What follows is a sampling of both
types of invasions.

—An assistant professor had a personal falling-out with the
dean of his graduate school. According to observers, the rift
had to do with an outside consulting assignment and did not
concern the professor's teaching or personal habits, both of
which were generally regarded as above criticism. The dean
vowed that the professor would never find a good job in
another university. To make sure, he inserted in the man's
file some fabricated assertions that he was a homosexual and
a possible danger to students. When the professor applied
for jobs elsewhere, he received what was (for him) an in-
explicable lack of interest in considering his application.

—While a sales supervisor was away on business, her boss

went through all the folders in her desk drawers and file cabinets, including those marked "Personal." Queried about this by another manager who happened to hear about it, the boss responded that the employee was believed to have some cost figures that would be useful. While judges have cautioned management that it has no right to prowl through an absent employee's desk on a fishing expedition, it appears that any pretext will suffice, so long as a senior manager does the prowling. In one case, this rule was upheld in court even though the employee's locked desk was pried open.[4]

—When one company recently decided, on its own initiative, to revise its personnel files in favor of more light, less secrecy, and better safeguards on use, it was discovered by an alert administrator that information on two employees with similar names—let us call them "Robert Anderson" and "Robert Andersen"—had become mixed, years earlier, as a result of carelessness. On each employee there were various items that could have been embarrassing. When inquiries came from insurance firms, credit agencies, and other such sources, the answers were based on the garbled data. Neither Robert Anderson nor Robert Andersen knew what was going on.

—In 1974 the American Civil Liberties Union did a report on privacy and computer data banks. The authors of the investigation concluded that California was "closer to 1984 than the rest of the nation." For instance, California was the first state to have a county clerk's office continuously bugged. Conversations that employees of the Los Angeles County Office in Pokona had with visitors were recorded because, according to the explanation of the county legal counsel, workers in that office "have no reasonable expectation of privacy."[5]

—In all but two states, company managers are free to monitor employees' conversations on company telephones without telling the employees. The two exceptions are California, which requires a beeper to be used on monitored phones, and Georgia, where the Public Service Commission requires that monitored phones be marked with a bright orange label and that monitoring supervisors obtain licenses.

—The Government Information Subcommittee of the U.S. House of Representatives found numerous government agencies monitoring secretly in 1970, but no federal legislation resulted. A great many companies apparently monitor secretly. As the House subcommittee concluded, electronic equipment for monitoring has become quite sophisticated, and an employee cannot know whether, to what extent, or for what purpose he or she is unwittingly sharing telephone calls with a supervisor or higher-up.

—Incidentally, there is no legal restriction on a supervisor's putting any notes thus gathered in the personnel folder of the individual monitored, locked up from that person's view but available to senior management people and, if organization policy allows, outside groups.

—In 1974 the *Wall Street Journal* reported that Combustion Engineering, its management incensed by a *Journal* article describing certain terms of nuclear power contracts negotiated by the company, was requiring officers and employees to submit to lie detector tests. "Do you know anybody at the *Wall Street Journal?*" was one question asked by the polygraph operator. "Did you give any information to anybody at the *Wall Street Journal?*" was another.[6]

—According to Ralph Nader, a U.S. Senate study in 1974 estimated that between 200,000 and 300,000 lie detector tests are administered each year in companies. Nader also reported that two surveys showed that the loyalty of about one worker in every five is checked by eavesdropping or other means.[7]

According to an old Chinese saying, the buyer needs a thousand eyes, the seller but one. Personnel officials apparently have another version of this thought. Some of them say: the employer needs a thousand eyes, the employee but one.

However, neither this philosophy nor the present law sit well with the public mood. It is becoming increasingly obvious that Americans, old and young alike, object to the no-privacy-is-good-policy tradition. Former Supreme Court Justice William O. Douglas once said, "The right to be let alone is indeed the beginning of all freedom." This statement comes close to mirroring the national mood.

For instance, many national legislators are disturbed by reports that there are nearly 900 federal data banks containing more than 1.25 billion records with personal information about individuals. The U.S. Senate Government Operations Committee and other Congressional committees have shown dismay over the sharing of information that goes on among federal agencies. Various groups of experts have been studying ways to control this situation. The Pentagon, after complaints about information filed on discharged military personnel, has agreed to omit from discharge papers certain coded data that previously permitted prospective employers to identify misfits, drug abusers, and alcoholics.

Universities and schools face a similar change in attitude. Responding to college students' complaints about secret information in their files, Congress in 1974 enacted a law giving students the right to inspect their records. In that same year, a schoolteacher who lost her job after the school superintendent, without her consent, obtained a doctor's report that she was pregnant, went to court and got reinstated. The federal court held that her privacy could not thus be invaded.

In the business sector the wind has been blowing in the same direction. Reacting to employees' complaints about alleged invasions of their privacy, unions have been protesting more vigorously. The AFL-CIO has mounted a drive against lie detectors; partly because of its pressure, thirteen states have laws prohibiting the use of lie detector tests for employees or prospective employees. Some leading companies have seized the initiative in changing their policies (more about this presently).

SOME PATHS TO PRIVACY

What guidelines might be suggested that would balance employee interests with employer needs? The question has two parts: (a) collection of information; (b) use of information already collected.

In drawing up the guidelines that follow, I have taken advantage of the innovative work of International Business Machines. According to Professor Alan Westin of Columbia University, perhaps no company has spent more management time and money on the privacy question than IBM. Its commitment to greater protection of employee interests began in the middle 1960s, and intensified when Frank T. Cary became board chairman in 1973. He has encouraged special exploratory task forces, training sessions, help from outside consultants, and other efforts; he has written directives to managers on standards to be followed.[8] "The privacy issue is IBM's issue," Cary says. "It is the large data processing systems that have made privacy so pressing an issue. Given the kind of business we're in, we ought not to sit back and let someone else take the lead in trying to do something about it."

First, what about the *collection and retention* of information? The rules that follow are proposed for all organizations, public or private. I make no attempt to state the rules in a legal manner so as to cover all quarks and possibilities, but only to make the general intent clear.

1. Management can collect and keep in its personnel files only those facts about employees that are required by law or that are necessary to manage operations. Thus, IBM's job application forms no longer ask for previous addresses, or whether the employee has relatives working for IBM, or about prior mental problems, or about convictions more than five years back, or about more recent criminal charges that did not result in conviction.

2. Performance evaluations more than three years old must be weeded out from an employee's file. Other out-of-

date information should also be removed on schedule. For instance, if an employee had a hassle over his expense account in February, 1970, why keep any notations made then by an irritated boss?

3. Employees are entitled to know what information about them is on file and how it is being used. As Cary notes, employees should understand that "there's no great mystery about it."

4. An employee is entitled to see *most* of the information on file about him or her. Only in this way can he share in the responsibility for accuracy. Of course, there is some information that management usually wishes to be withheld. An example is a confidential discussion of an opportunity for promotion that was never given, or a boss's personal reactions to an unusual request that an employee brought in for discussion.

In IBM's case, comments of supervisors and fellow workers about an employee's effort to correct an alleged grievance are not available for him to see, either. If this data were available, the company's "Open Door" procedure for appealing grievances would not work so well, management feels, for other employees would not provide the candid reactions needed in handling the case.

Since enactment of the Privacy Act of 1974, federal government employees have been entitled to examine their personnel files. The Privacy Protection Study Commission is investigating the need for further protection of personal information.

5. Employees' conversations (including telephone) and meetings may not be taped or monitored without their knowledge and consent.

6. A boss is not entitled to use *any* available means of checking up on an employee, say, to confirm a reason given for an absence, or to find out the reason for an unscheduled absence. For instance, calling the employee's home and "cross-examining" whoever answers the phone is not permissible. Neither is sending an investigator out to peer at

the home with binoculars, peep in the windows, or follow an employee on a trip.

7. Personality and general intelligence tests are not permissible. However, aptitude tests and skill tests may be legitimate, for they give an employer relevant knowledge about an applicant's ability. For example, typing tests may be given at IBM. At a company where delicate manual assembly is important, manual dexterity tests may be useful. At the *Harvard Business Review*, applicants for some editorial positions are given a "test article" to edit.

8. When an employee is absent or has left the organization, regular mail addressed to him may be opened only by a person in authority (e.g., his immediate boss or the personnel manager), and envelopes marked "Personal" may not be opened by anyone in the organization, unless the employee authorizes someone to do so.

9. When an employee is away, his desk and personal office files may be opened only by someone in authority who is looking for specific items of information needed for operations. For instance, it would be permissible for a boss to search for a letter containing a price quotation relevant to negotiations the boss is conducting. But if the boss's eye falls on some letters on another matter, as he hunts for the price quotation, he may not say, "Hm-m-m, these look interesting," and take them, too. Nor may he look through the employee's desk on a fishing expedition, that is, when he is not sure what he is after. In other words, we want to apply the principle of the Fourth Amendment, the guarantee in our Bill of Rights that a person's house may not be searched by officers without a warrant indicating why and for what evidence the search is being conducted.

10. It is not permissible to use polygraphs ("lie detectors") or psychological stress evaluators (PSEs) in interviewing applicants for jobs, candidates for transfer or promotion, or employees who may have knowledge of a problem being investigated, except with their permission. If they do not give permission, that decision must not be held against

them. It may be true, as the polygraph and PSE buffs insist, that the innocent person has nothing to fear. But the very mystique of these impersonal, police-type instruments makes them fearsome to many people. They look too much like a device of "pathological professionalism" in the personnel department.

11. If an employee's conversation is taped with his or her permission, the tape may not be run later through a PSE or other black plastic machine without his permission.

Now what about the *uses made* of information about employees on file? As indicated, what organizations do with the data may be as serious a breach of privacy as the manner of collection. I propose the following rules.

1. All information on file about an employee is confidential, and an employer may furnish no fact to an outsider without the employee's consent or a court order. In other words, the employer has a fiduciary relationship to the employee, much as a lawyer does to his client or a doctor to his patient. No distinction may be drawn (as some lawyers have suggested) between personnel information that is "tangible" property and information that is "intangible" property.

One of many advantages of such a clear and decisive rule is that an employee need have no fear of saying something in the employment interview, or in an interview for possible promotion, that he will regret later on. I recall the case of a corporate planner who confided in some detail to his prospective employer about an emotional problem he had, giving names of doctors, hospitals, and so on. His frankness helped him to get the position he wanted. However, several years later he became greatly concerned that the information might be made available to another organization that had inquired about him. "I'm killed if it is," he said.

2. Within the organization, the use of files must be classified. This is one of the principles IBM follows. It divides information about an employee into job-related files and personal information files. The employee's supervisors can see the first type of data, but they cannot look at the personal information files, which contain facts and statements about

medical insurance claims, life insurance beneficiaries, criminal convictions, wage garnishments, applications for home loan guarantees, and so forth. Only personnel officials can see this second type of data.

3. No information about an employee may be destroyed without his consent (unless the organization is simply following a standard procedure, such as the removal of out-of-date data mentioned earlier). The purpose of this rule is to prevent "mysterious disappearances" of information that might be helpful to an employee in a controversy.

Do these rules unfairly fetter management? They do make it more difficult for managers to get a "complete picture" of an employee. There are times when it would indeed be helpful, let us say, to a sales executive if he could see information in the personal information folder that he is forbidden to see, or if he could go back eight or ten years in the file and find "clues" to an employee's puzzling behavior. This is the debit side. However, on the credit side of the ledger is the importance of privacy. Many employees feel strongly about it, and a "bill of rights" would be reassuring.

Another debit is that outsiders may not be able to get information that would be quite helpful to them. In the example of the planning official, for instance, the facts about his mental illness would undoubtedly have been interesting to the outside group. But, again, the debit is offset by the value of greater privacy to individuals.

Also, it should be noted that these rules would not hobble management in security efforts. Where the checking of purses, briefcases, and bundles is legal today, it would still be legal. Moreover, where the law today authorizes a boss or employer to give frank opinions about an employee to an outsider, in answer to questions about the person's competence and character, those opinions could still be provided.

Finally, it is important to note that the main impact of these rules is not to reduce the amount of accurate, relevant, verifiable information available to bosses concerned with a person's on-the-job record. The main loss is of flimsy information. Arthur R. Miller was referring to commercial credit bureaus when he concluded, "The resulting reports usually contain hearsay narratives and off-the-cuff opinions gleaned from quick interviews with neighbors, landlords, employers and 'friends.' "[9] But he could have been referring to personnel folders on file in many other business and public organizations. One personnel executive reported that more than three-fourths of the comments about one employee recently reviewed came from persons who could no longer be contacted, and were apparently collected in haste. "It's impossible to read them without getting prejudiced against Mrs. ————," he remarked, "yet most of the stuff is unreliable and has nothing to do with her work here."

EMPLOYEES À LA MODE

Now let us turn from the privacy of information issue to the question of employee manners, dress, and life style. Few organizations want their staffs to look like students in a military academy, or bow and curtsy, or speak without splitting infinitives. At the same time, few managements feel indifferent about personal habits and style. Appearance can affect morale, customers, and public opinion. Sometimes, therefore, a line must be drawn. But where? And by whom?

In general, the law says that managers may set "reasonable" bounds for dress, hair styles, and grooming. For instance:

—A young man employed by a marketing research organization began reporting to work in colorful sport shirts and no neckties. When a supervisor told him he would have to wear a necktie, the employee refused and was fired. The employee went to court. The company had violated the Civil Rights Act, he charged—female employees were not required to wear ties. Also, the company was old-fashioned; many young men found ties uncomfortable and regarded them as outmoded. But in late 1975 a U.S. district court ruled in favor of the company. Considering the nature of its business—its need to appear "professional," the expectations of potential customers, and so forth—management was making only a reasonable demand when it insisted on neckties for male workers.[10]

—When a switchboard operator turned up at work wearing tattered, faded, soiled blue jeans, her supervisor exclaimed, "Really now! You ought to know better than that. We won't have it here." The operator said she felt more comfortable in jeans and refused to change. When told she had forfeited her job, she went to the union and began a grievance proceeding. Her case was built on the popularity of jeans among young women in 1975, her desire to be comfortable, and the fact that she could not be seen by the people whose calls she handled. Management countered with the belief that sales people, delivery men, customers, and others did on occasion pass through the switchboard area and get an impression of the company. Besides, it had a long-standing rule about dress which the operator knew about when she took the job. The arbitrator agreed with the company. The woman got her job back when she agreed to conform in the future, but she was not awarded back pay for the time she was laid off.[11]

—In 1974 Ken Kunes, the county assessor in Phoenix, Arizona, insisted that his female employees wear dresses. In 1975 he ordered male employees not to let their hair grow within one inch above the collar. Four men let their hair grow longer than that. Kunes fired them. The men went to court, claiming their rights of free expression had been violated. The court ruled in favor of Kunes; his order was reasonable.

—In 1975 the New Hampshire Supreme Court ruled that the New Hampshire State Hospital could require a security guard to shorten his hair as a condition of keeping his job. The guard had argued that his hair was neat and, though it came down to the level of his collar, was no longer than women's hair. The court did not agree with him that his rights of free expression were at stake.

Presumably most managers feel this general line of decisions by arbitrators and judges is sound. In my surveys of several thousand executives' opinions on employee rights, I found a heavy majority favoring restrictions of the type just described. These were the same liberal respondents who felt employees should be entitled to refuse to obey unethical orders and to speak out on issues of social responsibility where they disagreed with top management.

As civil liberties advocates have long noted, censorship is not only oppressive but it looks ridiculous when a historical perspective is taken. Today in Michigan mustaches are well accepted, even prized by many well-groomed men; yet in the early 1960s the case of a senior high student who chose to wear a neat mustache caused an uproar in Saginaw, Michigan.

Again, modern art was forbidden in many public halls not so long ago. Now it is a public relations plus for Chase Manhattan, Reynolds Tobacco, S. C. Johnson, and other well-known companies that buy and display expensive modern paintings and sculpture for all visitors to see. Books by James Joyce, Henry Miller, and other authors were forbidden distribution in the U.S. a few years ago because they were considered obscene. Now *The Joy of Sex* and *More Joy* are best-sellers in leading bookstores. One can go on and on with such examples.

Yet it is a fact that the people an organization serves, buys from, and does business with are affected by employee appearance. Whether these people's attitudes, and the censors who influence them, are rational or irrational is beside the point from an economic standpoint. The organization *can* be hurt. Keeping in mind that managers and organizations have rights which must be balanced against the rights of a dissident employee group, it would seem fair to accept intrusions like those described so long as there are solid checks and balances on management's power. In other words, the dissidents must have some effective way of challenging the intrusion.

Just as employees' hair styles and choice of clothes may be their own business, up to a point, so may their "personality styles"—their angers and frustrations, their feelings about alcohol and sex, their patriotism, and other attitudes. When does their own business become the organization's business?

For instance, a few years ago a supervisor in a state agency of California was sitting in a restaurant watching two other male employees dining with a female employee whom he much admired. When the men escorted the young lady to a motel room, the supervisor could stand his frustration no more. He jerked out a pistol and threatened to kill the two Lotharios if they did not stop "ruining" the young lady whom he so much admired. Next week the supervisor was fired. He petitioned to get his job back, going first to the state personnel board. There he lost on the ground that his conduct had a harmful effect on the staff. Next he went to the California Court of Appeals. Taking into account his record of long service, the court said that discharge was too severe a punishment. It gave him his job back.[12]

Sexual morality is a bottomless pit of problems. A competent employee with ten years of experience in one company happened to be a young woman who dated lots of men, including other workers. Her amours were a favorite subject of office gossip. On two occasions a jilted sweetheart stomped into her office and threatened her. Management got so irritated it told her to leave: She was a loose woman and a danger to morale. Rushing to her defense, the union claimed that her private life was her own business and that it was management's job to keep out intruders, not hers. When the case went to arbitration, the union's argument prevailed over management's and the young woman got her job back.[13]

However, the moment a person's life style becomes a possible threat to the organization as an economic whole—that is, to customer and public relations rather than to a group of employees—the decision is likely to go to management. For instance, a bank teller was called in one day and told that various customers had noticed him at a local bar early in the morning. The teller said yes, this was true, but he always got to work on time and did his job. But what would the bank's customers think? It was a small town, wasn't it? When the teller refused to change his habits, he was given a pink slip. Applying for unemployment compensation, the teller argued that his dismissal was not due to disobedience because the bank had no right to run his private life. The unemployment agency did not agree with him. When an employee's behavior affects the organization's image, controls are justified, the agency ruled.[14]

What about searching an employee's purse, carrying case, or other belongings when he or she comes to work or leaves? So long as the search is done in a reasonable way for an understandable purpose—plant security, for instance—the law says there is no invasion of privacy. In fact, in a recent arbitration case a Wisconsin coal mine company was allowed to have its supervisors "pat down" miners to see if prohibited smoking articles were being carried.[15]

The law today is characterized by its concern for the rights of owners, managers, creditors, and agents. This preoccupation is not wholly materialistic. Indeed, it is not completely inconsistent with humanistic concern for life, liberty, and individualism. For unless organizations survive and prosper, people cannot rise much above the subsistence level. Even the most liberal society must recognize this.

On the other hand, little is gained if organizations prosper while the souls within them vie, in John Donne's phrase, "to watch one another out of fear." In the long run no organization can achieve much at the expense of the quality of life in its offices, plants, and stores. This is why it is so important to extend and expand the right of privacy. Much more can be done before we need to worry about threatening the ability of managers to manage.

NOTES

1. Studs Terkel, *Working* (New York: Pantheon, 1974).
2. Mordechai Mironi, "The Confidentiality of Personnel Records: A Legal and Ethical View," *Labor Law Journal*, May 1974, p. 286.
3. Mironi, p. 273.
4. N.Y., U.I.A.B. Appeal #169,246. Also see *Protection Management* (New York, N.Y., Man & Manager), September 1, 1974.
5. *Boston Globe*, February 24, 1974, p. 8.
6. *Wall Street Journal*, March 21, 1974.
7. *New York Times*, May 9, 1976.
8. See "IBM's Guidelines to Employee Privacy," an interview with Frank T. Cary conducted by David W. Ewing and Wanda A. Lankenner, *Harvard Business Review*, September-October 1976, p. 82.
9. Arthur R. Miller, *The Assault on Privacy* (Ann Arbor: University of Michigan Press, 1971), p. 69.
10. 9 EPD Sec. 10, 197 (1975). Also see *White Collar Management* (New York, N.Y., Man & Manager), January 15, 1976.
11. 62 LA 1107 (1975). Also see *White Collar Management,* April 15, 1975.
12. 102 *Cal. Reporter* 50 (1972). Also see *White Collar Management,* January 1, 1973.
13. 67-1 ARB 3262 (1967). Also see *White Collar Management,* April 15, 1967.
14. N.Y., U.I.A.B. Appeal #A-750-1185 (1971). Also see *White Collar Management*, October 15, 1971.
15. *In re Wisconsin Steel Coal Mines*, June 30, 1976, 67 LA 84.

9

A
PROPOSED
BILL OF RIGHTS

What should a bill of rights for employees look like?

First, it should be presented in the form of clear and practical injunctions, not in the language of desired behavior or ideals.

In 1789, when James Madison and other members of the first U.S. Congress settled down to write the Bill of Rights (the first ten amendments to the Constitution), Madison insisted on using the imperative "shall" instead of the flaccid "ought," which had been used in the declarations of rights by the states, from which the ideas for the federal Bill of Rights were taken. For instance, where Virginia's historic Declaration of Rights of 1776 stated that "excessive bail ought not to be required," and where the amendments proposed in 1788 by Virginia legislators were identically worded, the amendment proposed by Madison (and later accepted) read: "Excessive bail shall not be required. . . ."

The imperative has precisely the same advantage in a bill of rights for members of a corporation, government bureau, university administration, or other organization. An analogy is a traffic light. It does not contain various shades of red but just one shade which means clearly and unequivocally, "Stop." Nor does a stop sign say "Stop If Possible" or "Stop If You Can." It says simply "Stop."

Second, as a general rule, it is wise to phrase a bill of rights in terms of negative injunctions rather than positive ones. A bill of rights does not aim to tell officials what they can do so much as it aims to tell them what they cannot do. It is not like the delegation of powers found in constitutions. Here again it is instructive to recall the writing of the federal Bill of Rights in 1789. Madison insisted that the positive grants of government powers had been well provided for in the main body of the Constitution and did not need to be reiterated in the first ten amendments.

In addition, a "Thou shalt not" type of commandment generally can be more precise than a "Thou shalt" type of commandment; the latter must be worded and interpreted to cover many possibilities of affirmative action. Since it is more precise, a "Thou shalt not" injunction is more predictable—not quite as predictable as a traffic light, but more so than most positive injunctions can be.

Also, since it is more limited, a negative injunction is less of a threat to the future use of executive (and legislative) powers. For instance, the injunction "Congress shall make no law respecting an establishment of religion" (first item in the U.S. Bill of Rights) inhibits Congress less, simply because it is so precise, than a positive command such as "Congress shall respect various establishments of religion" (rejected by the Founding Fathers when proposed in the 1789 discussions), which is more protean and expansible.

Third, an organization's bill of rights should be succinct. It should read more like a recipe in a cookbook than the regulations of the Internal Revenue Service. It is better to start with a limited number of rights that apply to familiar situations and that may have to be extended and amended in a few years than try to write a definitive listing for all time. Rights take time to ingest.

Fourth, a bill of rights should be written for understanding by employees and lay people rather than by lawyers and personnel specialists. It should not read like a letter from a credit company or a Massachusetts auto insurance policy. If an organization desires to make everything clear for experts, it could add a supplement or longer explanation that elaborates in technical terms on the provisions and clarifies questions and angles that might occur to lawyers.

Fifth, a bill of rights should be enforceable. Existence as a creed or statement of ideals is not enough. While creeds indeed may influence behavior in the long run, in the short run they leave too much dependent on good will and hope.

The bill of rights that follows is one person's proposal, a "working paper" for discussion, not a platform worked out in committee. As the short commentaries indicate, these proposed rights encapsulate parts of the discussion and reasoning in preceding chapters. The slight variations in style are purposeful—partly to reduce monotony and partly to suggest different ways of defining employee rights and management prerogatives.

1. *No organization or manager shall discharge, demote, or in other ways discriminate against any employee who criticizes, in speech or press, the ethics, legality, or social responsibility of management actions.*

Comment: This right is intended to extend the U.S. Supreme Court's approach in the *Pickering* case (Chapter 6) to all employees in business, government, education, and public service organizations.

What this right does not say is as important as what it does say. Protection does not extend to employees who make nuisances of themselves or who balk, argue, or contest managerial decisions on normal operating and planning matters, such as the choice of inventory accounting method, whether to diversify the product line or concentrate it, whether to rotate workers on a certain job or specialize them, and so forth. "Committing the truth," as Ernest Fitzgerald called it, is protected only for speaking out on issues where we consider an average citizen's judgment to be as valid as an expert's—truth in advertising, public safety standards, questions of fair disclosure, ethical practices, and so forth.

Nor does the protection extend to employees who malign the organization. We don't protect individuals who go around ruining other people's reputations, and neither should we protect those who vindictively impugn their employers.

Note, too, that this proposed right does not authorize an employee to disclose to outsiders information that is confidential.

This right puts publications of nonunionized employees on the same basis as union newspapers and journals, which are free to criticize an organization. Can a free press be justified for one group but not for the other? More to the point still, in a country that practices democratic rites, can the necessity of an "underground press" be justified in any socially important organization?

2. *No employee shall be penalized for engaging in outside activities of his or her choice after working hours, whether political, economic, civic, or cultural, nor for buying products and services of his or her choice for personal use, nor for expressing or encouraging views contrary to top management's on political, economic, and social issues.*

Comment: Many companies encourage employees to participate in outside activities, and some states have committed this right to legislation. Freedom of choice of products and services for personal use is also authorized in various state statutes as well as in arbitrators' decisions. The third part of the statement extends the protection of the First Amendment to the employee whose ideas about government, economic policy, religion, and society do not conform with the boss's. It would also protect the schoolteacher who allows the student newspaper to espouse a view on sex education that is rejected by the principal (for example, the Joan Lentczner case mentioned in Chapter 6), the staff psychologist who endorses a book on a subject considered taboo in the board room, and other independent spirits.

Note that this provision does not authorize an employee to come to work "beat" in the morning because he or she has been moonlighting. Participation in outside activities should enrich employees' lives, not debilitate them; if on-the-job performance suffers, the usual penalties may have to be paid.

3. *No organization or manager shall penalize an employee for refusing to carry out a directive that violates common norms of morality.*

Comment: The purpose of this right is to take the rule of the *Zinman* case a step farther and afford job security (not just unemployment compensation) to subordinates who cannot perform an action because they consider it unethical or illegal. It is important that the conscientious objector in such a case hold to a view that has some public acceptance. Fad moralities—messages from flying saucers, mores of occult religious sects, and so on—do not justify refusal to carry out an order. Nor in any case is the employee entitled to interfere with the boss's finding another person to do the job requested.

4. *No organization shall allow audio or visual recordings of an employee's conversations or actions to be made without his or her prior knowledge and consent. Nor may an organization require an employee or applicant to take personality tests, polygraph examinations, or other tests that constitute, in his opinion, an invasion of privacy.*

Comment: This right is based on policies that some leading organizations have already put into practice. If an employee doesn't want his working life monitored, that is his privilege so long as he demonstrates (or, if an applicant, is willing to demonstrate) competence to do a job well.

5. *No employee's desk, files, or locker may be examined in his or her absence by anyone but a senior manager who has sound reason to believe that the files contain information needed for a management decision that must be made in the employee's absence.*

Comment: The intent of this right is to grant people a privacy right as employees similar to that which they enjoy as political and social citizens under the "searches and seizures" guarantee of the Bill of Rights (Fourth Amendment to the Constitution). Many leading organizations in business and government have respected the principle of this rule for some time.

6. *No employer organization may collect and keep on file information about an employee that is not relevant and necessary for efficient management. Every employee shall have the right to inspect his or her personnel file and challenge the accuracy, relevance, or necessity of data in it, except for personal evaluations and comments by other employees which could not reasonably be obtained if confidentiality were not promised. Access to an employee's file by outside individuals and organizations shall be limited to inquiries about the essential facts of employment.*

Comment: This right is important if employees are to be masters of their employment track records instead of possible victims of them. It will help to eliminate surprises, secrets, and skeletons in the clerical closet.

7. *No manager may communicate to prospective employers of an employee who is about to be or has been discharged gratuitous opinions that might hamper the individual in obtaining a new position.*

Comment: The intent of this right is to stop blacklisting. The courts have already given some support for it.

8. *An employee who is discharged, demoted, or transferred to a less desirable job is entitled to a written statement from management of its reasons for the penalty.*

Comment: The aim of this provision is to encourage a manager to give the same reasons in a hearing, arbitration, or court trial that he or she gives the employee when the cutdown happens. The written statement need not be given unless requested; often it is so clear to all parties why an action is being taken that no document is necessary.

9. *Every employee who feels that he or she has been penalized for asserting any right described in this bill shall be entitled to a fair hearing before an impartial official, board, or arbitrator. The findings and conclusions of the hearing shall be delivered in writing to the employee and management.*

Comment: This very important right is the organizational equivalent of due process of law as we know it in political and community life. Without due process in a company or agency, the rights in this bill would all have to be enforced by outside courts and tribunals, which is expensive for society as well as time-consuming for the employees who are required to appear as complainants and witnesses. The nature of a "fair hearing" is purposely left undefined here so that different approaches can be tried, expanded, and adapted to changing needs and conditions.

Note that the findings of the investigating official or group are not binding on top management. This would put an unfair burden on an ombudsperson or "expedited arbitrator," if one of them is the investigator. Yet the employee is protected. If management rejects a finding of unfair treatment and then the employee goes to court, the investigator's statement will weigh against management in the trial. As a practical matter, therefore, employers will not want to buck the investigator-referee unless they fervently disagree with the findings.

In Sweden, perhaps the world's leading practitioner of due process in organizations, a law went into effect in January 1977 that goes a little farther than the right proposed here. The new Swedish law states that except in unusual circumstances a worker who disputes a dismissal notice can keep his or her job until the dispute has been decided by a court.

Every sizable organization, whether in business, government, health, or another field, should have a bill of rights for employees. Only small organizations need not have such a statement—personal contact and oral communications meet the need for them. However, companies and agencies need not have identical bills of rights. Industry custom, culture, past history with employee unions and associations, and other considerations can be taken into account in the wording and emphasis given to different provisions.

For instance, Booz, Allen and Hamilton, the well-known consulting company, revised a bill of rights for its employees in 1976 (the list included several of the rights suggested here). One statement obligated the company to "Respect the right of employees to conduct their private lives as they choose, while expecting its employees' public conduct to reflect favorably upon the reputation of the Firm." The latter part of this provision reflects the justifiable concern of a leading consulting firm with outward appearances. However, other organizations—a mining company, let us say, or a testing laboratory—might feel no need to qualify the right of privacy because few of their employees see customers.

In what ways can due process be assured? There are certain procedures that the organization itself can establish. These will be described in the next two chapters. In addition, society can undertake to assure due process for employees. This avenue will be described in Chapter 12.

PART IV

STEPS TO CONSTITUTIONALISM

The individual must be re-created in the light
of a revivified humanism which sets the value
of man the unique against that vast and ominous
shadow of man the composite, the predictable,
which is the delight of the machine.

—Loren Eiseley

10

MAKING
DUE PROCESS
A
REALITY

Although the notion of an employee bill of rights is attractive to many Americans, they wonder how it could be enforced. Wouldn't hostile bosses be able to circumvent it in subtle ways? For instance, they could discharge, demote, or penalize the employee for trumped-up errors. They could reduce the scope of the job, or perhaps prune it to death, thereby making the employee "unnecessary." Using their superior communication channels, they could spread false rumors about the person's poor performance. And if it were possible to get solid evidence about such retaliation (often it is not possible), the day of reckoning might be so long in coming, because of the log jam of legal and arbitration cases, that the penalty might have no deterrent value for vindictive supervisors.

In short, a bill of rights by itself is not enough. Ways must be found to put the employee on the same level as the boss whenever differences of opinion arise over the exercise of rights. Only if such ways are found can it be said that constitutionalism exists. Commenting on free speech, Walter Lippman once observed: "While the right to talk may be the beginning of freedom, the necessity of listening is what makes the right important."

There are two requirements for constitutionalism: first,

that the rights themselves be clearly defined; second, that satisfactory means exist to enforce them equitably. The last word is an important condition of due process of law. As the great jurist Learned Hand once said, "To keep our democracy, there must be one commandment: Thou shalt not ration justice."

What should due process mean in an organization? Here are the main requirements:

1. It must be a procedure; it must follow rules. It must not be arbitrary. In the movie *The Green Berets* John Wayne says, "Out here due process is a bullet." In a large number of organizations until now, due process has been less violent but not much more subtle. "In this place due process is a pink slip," many employees might say. There must be no justification for such cynicism.

2. It must be visible, well-known enough so that potential violators of rights and victims of abuse know of it.

3. It must be predictably effective. Employees must have confidence that previous decisions in favor of rights will be repeated.

4. It must be "institutionalized." That is, it must be a relatively permanent fixture in the organization, not a device that is here today, gone tomorrow. Also, it must be a wheel that makes other wheels turn, not one that turns by itself; when a case is decided one way or the other, the organization must take heed.

5. It must be perceived as equitable. The standards used in judging a case must be respected and accepted by a majority of employees, bosses as well as subordinates. They must feel that due process expresses their own feelings about what is equitable.

6. It must be easy to use. Employees must be able to understand it without fear that procedural complexities will get the best of them.

7. It must apply to all employees. The lowest-paid person who "commits the truth" is entitled to the same treatment as a scientist, computer expert, or executive.

Due process does *not* have to be legal in the sense that it is enforced by the courts, arbitration agencies, or other outside authorities. It does *not* have to be the same in detail from one organization to another. Richard Walton has noted: "Wide variations exist in the extent to which the organizational culture respects personal privacy, tolerates dissent, adheres to high standards of equity in distributing rewards, and provides for due process in all work-related matters."[1] The exact procedure used by a company or agency can reflect such differences, even though certain basic principles of equitable review may be followed everywhere.

Is the idea of due process for employees consistent with the American mood? In most states, prisoners are winning rights to due process; forty-one states permit cross-examination and some legal representation in prison disciplinary proceedings. Students have sought and won due process in many parts of the country. "Young people do not shed their rights at the schoolhouse door," said the U.S. Supreme Court in 1975, ruling that pupils cannot be suspended without an explanation of the evidence against them and an opportunity to respond.[2]

Especially important is the trend in management thinking. In my *Harvard Business Review* survey of attitudes toward the rights of employees, I found that three-fourths of the 3,400 respondents believed an about-to-be fired employee was entitled to know all the accusations against his or her performance.[3] Although that right is only part of what due process is all about, surely it shows how the mood is shifting from the days when managers considered themselves free to move employees out, in, and around at will.

COMPANY "COURTS": JUSTICE DOESN'T HAVE TO BE LEGISLATED

A few pioneering organizations have experimented with informal, nonlegal "courts" for reviewing cases of alleged injustice. These courts take the complaint *before* the aggrieved employee has been fired, demoted, or in some other way penalized. The employee may be entitled to "counsel" to present his or her case—not necessarily an attorney but at least an executive who is articulate, knowledgeable, and able to present the defense sympathetically. In the *Harvard Business Review* survey, 6 percent of the respondents reported that their organizations had a "hearing procedure that allows the employee to be represented by an attorney or other counsel, and with a neutral company executive deciding on the evidence."

The informal company or agency court has two enormous advantages. First, it can act quickly. The aggrieved employee doesn't grow old waiting for his turn for a hearing, as Michael Holodnak reportedly did in his legal hassle with Avco (see Chapter 6). Second, the decision serves as an instructive example to employees at all levels. If the grievance is rejected, bosses who are worrying about "what will they tie me up with next" are reassured. If the aggrieved employee is upheld, on the other hand, the organization gets a warning signal which, hopefully, will help it to steer clear of such errors in the future. In other words, people get feedback in time for it to be helpful.

Disadvantages? About half of the *Harvard Business Review* survey respondents rated the hearing procedure as low in effectiveness. Why? One reason, we may surmise, is simply that some managers view the "court" as a threat to their freedom to use their discretion. Another reason may be the importance to some managers of getting an offensive employee out of the organization immediately; in their view, a delay even of several weeks may mean that the employee stays on the premises long enough to "bad-mouth" management and prejudice other people. Significantly, the efforts of U.S. Civil Service executives to permit hearings to be held after a federal civil servant has been dismissed, rather than before, prevailed in April 1974; the U.S. Supreme Court ruled that it is not a violation of the due process clause of the Fifth Amendment to hold the hearing after dismissal.

Here is an example of a company hearing system.

Case of the Padded Hotel Bills. A company called California Products (fictitious name) had printed regulations entitling a discharged employee to request and obtain a hearing, ordinarily within fourteen days of the request.[4] An assistant supervisor named "Carol Stanton" was fired by her boss for altering her hotel bills on a trip to Los Angeles to recruit employees. She admitted that she had changed a charge of $9 to $19, and a bill for $4 to $64, but she insisted this was done to make up for out-of-pocket business costs she could not bill the company for, under its regulations. She insisted that discharge was too severe a penalty and requested a hearing.

At the hearing, the personnel vice-president presided. Another man presented Stanton's case for her; a third man, an industrial relations manager, presented the company's case. A stenographer was present to record what went on. In addition, the presiding officer asked several other company people to be on hand as "resources."

First, Stanton's counsel brought out her side of the case. He asked questions about her background and thirteen-year service at California Products. He elicited her explanation of why she felt justified in padding her expense account.

Next, the company's "attorney" presented management's case; he questioned Stanton at some length. Then the hearing officer asked the "resource" people to testify about their knowledge of Stanton's service, the company's expense account regulations, and related matters. At the end, the company and Stanton's counsel summed up their sides of the case briefly.

After the hearing, the stenographer typed up the transcript for the presiding officer. He reflected on the case and, in the ten days, rendered his decision. He ruled that Stanton should not be discharged but should be reinstated in a lower position at reduced pay. He reasoned that her long period of faithful and competent service entitled her to less Draconian treatment. He also ordered her to return to the company the amount she had overcharged it, and gave her a temporary suspension without pay.

After the decision was announced, the company president vented his unhappiness with it in a letter to the hearing officer, *but he let the decision stick.* The president also sent a strong letter to all branch offices saying the decision should not be interpreted as condoning dishonesty.

This kind of company "court" system could afford potent protection for such employee rights as speech, privacy, conscience, and independence of choice in after-hours activities. Suppose, for example, that Stanton's discharge had followed an argument with her boss over a fishing expedition he had conducted through her files while she was away on the recruiting trip, or over some criticisms of misleading company advertising she had voiced at a cocktail party. Her rights could have been protected before real damage was done, had they been set forth in a company bill of rights and been accepted by the "court." The decision would have served as a concrete example to everyone of what was not a justifiable discharge and why.

Also significant in the California Products case is the chief executive's willingness to accept the "court's" decision even though he didn't like it. In our political system there is no due process unless the executive arm of government supports the decisions of the judicial arm. Similarly, in an organization due process means that management backs the decisions of the review panel.

The right to "counsel" is another important feature of the system described. In one case, a hospital orderly took a problem with his boss to a senior official, as prescribed in the hospital handbook. Because the orderly lacked the ability to plead his case—he tended to get tongue-tied when excited—he got another employee to act as his "counsel." But the senior official refused to listen to the "counsel," insisting that the orderly speak for himself. Dismayed, the orderly dropped his appeal. Soon afterward, both he and his friend quit their jobs at the hospital.

OTHER COMPANIES' REVIEW PROCEDURES

How have other companies approached the need for due process? Here are two brief examples:

—H. P. Hood Company in Boston provides a written statement of its hearing procedure. According to researchers A. R. Evans and Mark J. Thomas, if any one of Hood's 3,100 nonunionized employees feels that his or her supervisor has been unfair, then talks with the supervisor and gets no satisfaction, he is encouraged to go to a manager higher up or to the personnel department. If he still can't get a fair solution, in his opinion, the employee is encouraged to go to the company president, who will appoint a panel of five nonmanagement employees, chosen at random, to gather facts on the grievance. With this report in hand, the president renders a decision in the presence of the aggrieved person and the boss.[5]

—Polaroid Corporation, with about 12,000 nonunionized employees, has a committee whose job is to represent an employee who has a grievance. This is done in a hearing before representatives of management. The committee members are elected from the ranks. Evans and Thomas report that a fair number of management decisions are overruled in the hearings. If the decision goes against the aggrieved employee, he or she is entitled by company rules to submit the case to an outside arbitrator.[6]

The foregoing contrast sharply with what happens in a company that practices unilateral, unreviewed punishment. Here is the description of Louis V. McIntire, the chemical engineer whose case was mentioned in Chapter 6, given in an address to the American Association for the Advancement of Science in Boston, February 19, 1976:

> You are called into top management's office. This usually results in your standing alone and facing two or more management people. Your immediate supervisor is usually absent. Top management says your performance is not good. You protest that it is good. The management people suggest you might

be better off somewhere else and that you should leave the company quietly. They always point out that if you leave quietly, you can expect good recommendations. They also state that if you do not leave quietly and "voluntarily," then— "Well, you know what that means. . . ." You ask for management to give you their position in writing. Management refuses to give you anything in writing.

ARBITRATION AT VARIABLE SPEEDS

It is curious that arbitration lacks glamour in the public mind. People know about it and respect it, but somehow it lacks what Madison Avenue would call an "image." In thousands and thousands of workplaces, however, arbitration is what makes the difference between equity—and, equally important, overall employee confidence in equity—and injustice.

Perhaps one reason arbitration lacks an exciting image is its association with organized labor. Four workers out of five do not belong to traditional industrial and craft unions, and in the South and Southwest especially, employer resistance to unions remains strong. (According to A. H. Raskin, in 1974, some forty years after passage of the Wagner Act guaranteeing freedom to organize, about half of the 20,000 unfair labor practice charges filed against employers in field offices of the National Labor Relations Board involved accusations that workers had been dismissed for union activity.[7])

However, arbitration should be associated also with professional associations and unions of professionals, and their influence and power are gaining impressively. About 3 million members of unions and employee associations are classified as professionals; they include engineers, journalists, teachers, actors, and doctors.[8] Many close observers believe that scientists and other technical people will be the next to organize, overcoming their traditional suspicions of unions. If so, they too will be calling arbitration into play. Moreover, independent employee unions may support ar-

bitration, and, as we know from the Polaroid example just
mentioned, arbitration may exist even where there is no
semblance of employee organization.

Managerial unions, too, may be in the offing. This would
give another boost to arbitration. [Although managerial
unions received a setback in the Supreme Court's refusal in
1974 to put them under the umbrella of collective bargaining statutes, many close observers are convinced that their
growth is inevitable]

[What is exciting about arbitration is its potential for protecting speech, privacy, ethical integrity, and other vital
liberties. To be sure, to date it has been preoccupied with
productivity, work rules, bargaining rights, work loads, and
similar matters. But, as we shall see, its scope can be
stretched]

Case of the contrite critic.[9] A quality control inspector of
a company with government contracts accused the company
of fraud at a union meeting. According to management witnesses, he claimed the company was selling ammunition
that was not being inspected, and that bad material was
getting by. When confronted with these charges, the inspector denied making some of the statements, and he said that if
he did make them, he was sorry. But the company fired him
anyway.

The union took the case to arbitration (the union's contract
with the company contained provisions for hearings before
employee discharge). An attorney from the Federal Mediation and Conciliation Service took charge. After hearing both
sides of the case, he decided that the inspector had indeed
made the accusations. However, the inspector had done
competent work for the company for eleven years.
Moreover, there was no evidence his accusations had
caused harm to the organization. Therefore the arbitrator
felt that discharge was too harsh a penalty. He ordered the
inspector reinstated on the job, without back pay for the
three months he had been suspended.

In this organization's by-laws, employee rules, and union
contract there was no bill of rights protecting speech, yet

the quality control critic was protected. For most organizations, however, a bill of rights is needed to make the issues clear and assure a better guarantee of due process.

Is there any reason that employee unions or associations cannot write civil liberties into the contract? Apparently this step has not yet been taken. Judging from the general trend in collective bargaining, however, there seems to be no reason that it cannot be done—and the movement is unmistakably in this direction. For example, unions have been going outside the conventional scope of work conditions and dealing with problems of sexism in the office. Thus, the Screen Actors Guild has written into its contract a clause prohibiting prospective employers from interviewing actors and actresses outside the office (in a motel room, for instance). Also, unions are becoming ever more conscious of the rights of minorities, as spelled out in the Fourteenth and Fifteenth Amendments to the Constitution. If union officials consider rights like these important, surely they can add others to the list.

Expedited arbitration. One weakness of conventional arbitration is that it may take too long. In the case just cited, the quality control inspector was in limbo for three months while arbitration was arranged and conducted. The average arbitration proceeding takes from two to six months (from submission to hearing). Must the employee whose privacy has been invaded maliciously, or who has been fired or demoted for refusing to follow an unethical directive, wait so long for his or her rights to be asserted? If he has been discharged, he has no regular paycheck during that period and he may be ineligible for unemployment compensation. If he is not discharged, the boss may make every hour on the job miserable for him.

For reasons like these, the AFL-CIO passed a resolution, at its convention in Miami in 1974, calling on all of its 131 affiliates to lend a willing ear to any management proposals for expedited arbitration. That same year, General Electric and companies in the steel industry began a three-year experiment in expedited arbitration.

Under this approach, an impartial referee is called in immediately, makes his findings right away, and renders a decision in, say, a week. Thus, if a supervisor is accused of goring an assistant in some way, he must defend his actions practically on the spot. While the arbitrator may not catch the wrongdoer *in flagrante delicto*, he arrives while the blood is still fresh. If he cannot resolve the case at once, he will recommend a more formal hearing with witnesses, evidence, and spokesmen lined up in the usual fashion.

Expedited arbitration thus has great deterrent value. If you run the risk of hanging for a crime within twenty-four hours or seven days, you are more likely not to do it than if the day of reckoning is months or more away. Just as important, a swift judgment is more likely to brake the "problem employee" who, upset by some imagined persecution by a senior person, begins shouting accusations. Indeed, it would not be surprising if this device often turns out to be a strong friend of management.

The American Arbitration Association maintains a panel of more than 2,000 lawyers, civic leaders, and college professors who are able to make fast and fair judgments in disputes. The Federal Mediation and Conciliation Service has a similar setup; it even uses a computer in order to provide the disputing parties with a referee possessing the right technical and personality qualifications to suit them.

What are the weaknesses of arbitration as a form of due process? One is that most of the work is being done by a small number of experts. Lawrence Stessin estimates that about 400 referees are handling 90 percent of the cases. The fact that most of these people are veterans has prompted one observer to quip that "three dozen heart attacks could wipe out the system."

A second weakness is union management. While many unions are run by energetic, capable, and high-minded officials, other unions seem to be as despotic and corrupt as the worst corporate management teams. Run by mossbacks who couldn't care less about ideals like due process, these unions are not likely to feed a hawk that may come to prey in their own barnyard. In Congressional hearings over the years, witnesses have left no doubt that union organizations are subject to the same managerial diseases as other types of organizations. It remains to be seen whether the new generation of union officials will try to change all this.

Another question is internal union administration. Aggrieved insiders in the trade union movement are challenging their organizations just as corporate and government employees have. For instance, an official of a carpenters' union in Los Angeles brought a damage suit against it, charging that he was victimized by officers with whom he disagreed. He claimed that, following a disagreement over some administrative matters, he was subjected to a "campaign of intimidation" that included threats, public ridicule, verbal abuse, and job discrimination. The carpenter received an award of $182,500 from a jury. (The jurisdiction of the state trial court was questioned in the appeal; the U.S. Supreme Court decided in favor of the official.[10])

Some unions have already set up some form of due process. For instance, the United Auto Workers has a procedure allowing a member to appeal, to an impartial judge, certain official actions or decisions that seem to him to be onerous.

OMBUDSPEOPLE: AN OMNIBUS ANSWER

In *Areopagitica,* written more than three centuries ago in defense of English freedom, John Milton referred to an Egyptian legend about truth. Truth came into the world with her divine master, according to the legend. But after the master and his apostles left, the ignoble Typhon and his conspirators captured the virgin Truth. They "hewed her lovely form into a thousand pieces, and scattered them to the four winds. From that time ever since, the sad friends of Truth, such as dare appear, . . . went up and down gathering up limb by limb . . . still as they could find them."

When an employee in a public, educational, or business organization is persecuted and discriminated against for asserting his or her rights, the truth tends to get decimated and scattered to the winds like Truth in the Egyptian legend. The boss dissembles. Records and memoranda suddenly "disappear." The abused employee becomes distraught and says things he or she shouldn't. The employee's job is altered and the boss "learns" about past failures that somehow had been "kept from my attention." Given weird or difficult assignments, the employee stumbles. Before long the clouded situation is beyond clarification. Are the boss's claims of poor performance legitimate? Or are they just an excuse to punish the employee and teach other subordinates a lesson?

If the organization has an ombudsperson, it has an ingenious agency for handling difficult questions like these. The ombudsperson lacks formal powers and set procedures. There is no line authority here—no power to hire, fire, promote, transfer, give orders, or render a decision that binds management. Yet the ombudsperson is a Typhon-killer. He or she listens, investigates, informs, counsels, persuades, and recommends. If all this fails and clout must be used against an obstinate or ruthless supervisor, the order comes not from the ombudsperson but from a senior manager. An ombudsperson tries at all costs to avoid court fights and lawyers. "We lose even if we win," says one I know, referring to the long delays and high costs of litigation, and the bad publicity for the organization.

In addition, ombudspeople go without two common symbols of status and power: staffs and paperwork. They eschew staffs because, as Robert H. Gudger, formerly the ombudsman in Xerox's Information Technology Group, once noted, "People want to see the ombudsman himself, not an investigator or some other intermediary." And they eschew paperwork because, partly owing to the lack of assistants, they can't afford it.

"Ombudsman" is a Swedish word meaning attorney or representative. Sweden instituted an ombudsman in 1809. In that country he is appointed for a term and reports directly to Parliament. The idea is a comparatively recent export to the United States (where the term *ombudsperson* is preferred) and has been publicized more in government settings than in industry. Various state governments have created ombudspeople. In Minnesota and other states, ombudsperson offices have been set up for prisons. Giant Food and other retailers have made themselves more consumer-conscious by employing ombudspeople to represent customers.

According to management consultant Mack Hanan, the ombudsperson approach was first tried in industry during the 1960s in high-technology companies, science-based service organizations, and interdisciplinary "think tanks."[11] Among other manufacturers, according to Hanan, the ombudsperson is seen more often at the plant level than at any other. For example, Grumman Aerospace Corporation had a "plant coordinator" at more then thirty plants who dealt with all types of problems faced by employees.

Since there are no rights to privacy, due process, ethical independence, and free speech and press in most organizations, there are no reported examples of ombudspeople correcting injustice of the type we are concerned with in this book. But the successes they have had leave no doubt that they are well-equipped to handle such problems.

For example, in one recent case the ombudsperson of a large scientific organization investigated complaints that a manager was making sexual forays on his secretaries. After verifying the complaints by obtaining depositions from several secretaries who had been fired after resisting, none of whom knew the others, the ombudsperson brought the evidence to the head of the organization, who talked with the manager the next day and obtained his resignation.

Ombudspeople have been effective in combating subtle, surreptitious, sometimes unconscious abuses of assistants and subordinates. An insecure boss harasses assistants whom he fears may displace him, giving them extra work loads, refusing normally given permissions to attend professional meetings, and maligning them in conferences. A member of a minority group may be humiliated repeatedly by a colleague or department head. No one of these abuses or harassments by itself is actionable; some of them may not even be conscious, reflecting a bias the boss is not aware of. But they are insufferable for the victims and disastrous for general morale.

The peculiar power of the ombudsperson is that, so long as the abusive behavior offends the standards of normal, decent people, he or she does not need to prove illegality or violation of an employment contract. It is enough to sort out the evidence, discuss it with the people directly involved, and, if necessary, take it to a top executive with a recommendation. The support of top management is essential.

At Xerox, the ombudsman reports to the president of the division. The president is the only one who can reverse the ombudsman's decisions. Under the Xerox system, an aggrieved employee must first try to solve his problem through his supervisor or the personnel department. If that fails, the employee can submit a written complaint to the ombudsman. The system was started out of concern that the facts about a problem tended to get obnubilated when reported up the line. "If the first-line manager handles a situation poorly but fills out the forms neatly," said James P. O'Neill, head of the division, "by the time this gets four levels up the organization, nobody can tell what's wrong."

According to Mary P. Rowe, one of two ombudspeople at Massachusetts Institute of Technology who report to the president and chancellor, ombudspeople can be especially effective in sorting out the minutiae of sexism. " These minutiae are usually not actionable; most are such petty incidents that they may not even be identified, much less protected," says Rowe. " They are, however, important, like the dust and ice in Saturn's rings, because, taken together, they constitute formidable barriers. As Saturn is partially obscured by its rings, so are good jobs partially obscured for women by 'grains of sand': the minutiae of sexism."[12]

In the *Harvard Business Review* surveys of employee rights, less than one respondent in ten reported that his company had an ombudsperson, but nearly two-thirds of this minority rated the person high or medium-high in effectiveness.[13] Some of the companies employing ombudspeople are pace-setters in employee relations—for instance, General Electric and the Boeing Vertol division of the Boeing Company—and so it is likely that this practice will spread.

WORK COUNCILS AND ADVISORY BOARDS

"Man is more molecular than atomic," Judge Charles Wyzanski once noted. "It is in combination that man is effective."

There may be certain needs for due process that are better satisfied by boards and councils than by an ombudsperson, an arbitrator, or an informal hearing procedure. Boards and councils may lack the speed and fact-finding capacity of the other agencies. On the other hand, they have great political strength. In addition, a representative body is likely to enjoy high visibility. It may act late, as a result of debate and disagreement, but when it does act its decisions get well-reported through the organization.

At Xerox, this agency takes the form of formal employee advisory boards which study and make recommendations to top management on problems ranging from minority relations and women's rights to sales and philanthropic contributions. The boards have rotating memberships, and the members come from all over the organization. According to chief executive Peter McColough, in 1975, the boards were proving to be valuable, and management intended to expand their use, decentralizing them as much as possible so as to draw deeper on employee opinion.

Such boards can be found in other U.S. companies as well as in universities. Although usually called "advisory," they may be quite influential. Clearly they could be as effective with employee rights questions as with problems of administration and productivity.

Perhaps the most interesting examples of representative employee agencies in the English-speaking world come from England (which in turn seems to have adapted the concept from Scandinavia). These agencies differ from the advisory board model in that they are minilegislatures and, under the company-union contract or company by-laws, have institutional permanence. Let us consider three examples.

At each major geographical unit of Britain's Glacier Metal Company, there is a works council which develops written company policies and "standing orders" on such topics as overtime, night shifts, changes in working methods, plant closings, and wages and salaries. Members of the union elect the council members. Seven shop stewards join with three members of the clerical and/or other staffs, two middle-level staff people, one representative of the senior staff, and the chief executive of the local organization. The council meets at least once a month, and employees who want to watch the proceedings are admitted to a "stranger's gallery." The topics to be discussed are proposed by council members.[14] Rights of speech, privacy, and conscience have not been discussed so far as I know, but they could fit on the agenda any time.

Glacier Metal is a productive, successful company with 5,000 employees. It has been an innovator in industrial relations for some time and even has a written constitution under which all groups in the company renounce the right to impose changes in policy by unilateral action. Constitutionalism has by no means been a panacea for the company—the chief executive feels that various problems in communication and organization persist. On the other hand, it has led unmistakably to a quality of governance that is not unlike what an English or American citizen experiences in political life.

The second example of a company with a representative employee agency is the wool manufacturing concern of J. Newson & Son, Batley, Yorkshire. Its works council is composed of ten employee representatives, one foreman, four managers, and the managing director (who is the only one who doesn't vote). It has access to all company accounts and records except individual salaries. The works council has a number of triumphs to its credit, including putting through changes in working methods that other companies in the area have failed to enact peacefully. Another notable feature of the council is that voting does not split down the middle between management and nonmanagement council members; rather, members say that cross-voting is common. Although the works council is advisory in name, none of its recommendations has been rejected in thirteen years.

While the company has no bill of rights, and there is no record of "legislation" on rights questions like those described in this book, it seems clear that such matters could be taken up by the works council any time it wanted to.

The third example is Firestone Tyre and Rubber Company, in Bradford. Three elected shop stewards and a member of the industrial relations department (who acts as a neutral chairman) meet with the department head and foreman who are concerned with a case of disciplinary action. The committee meets about twice a month. It has power to impose a wide range of sanctions, from giving a warning to a problem employee to firing him or her. The company has a union (Transport and General Workers). The factory has not suffered from a strike over dismissal or suspension since the disciplinary committee was set up.

If an employee complained of abusive treatment because of exercising rights of free speech, privacy, or conscience, his complaint could go to the disciplinary committee without necessitating any change in its scope or procedures.

DE-INSTITUTIONALIZING INDIFFERENCE

Due process is a way of fighting institutionalized indifference to the individual—the indifference that says productivity and efficiency are the goals of an organization, and any person who stands in the way must be sacrificed. Too frequently a young man or woman joins a profit-hungry company or zealous public service agency and gradually acquires the uneasy feeling that other employees do not care, really care, about any person, even the boss. Then one day, with growing alarm, the employee realizes that it is the organization, and not only the organization but the whole economic and regulatory system, that does not care; and not merely that it does not care, but it doesn't care one way or the other.

Due process is the opposite of such indifference. It is institutionalized *caring.* "The worst sin towards our fellow creatures is not to hate them," George Bernard Shaw wrote in *The Devil's Desciple,* "but to be indifferent to them."

Unfortunately, due process is not a perfect answer to the question of how employee rights can be protected in a hierarchal, tough-minded, productivity-conscious company or public agency. For instance, if the woman in the California Products case had been appealing a right, say, to refuse to obey an unethical directive, her boss might have been able to make life miserable for her in ways that even this company's informal court system could not identify, after she went back to the job. If in one of the steel companies that is using expedited arbitration an employee is saved from unfair treatment by an arbitrator who flies in to get the facts and makes a swift judgment, the irritated boss may still succeed in venting his frustrations on the subordinate in subtle ways after the arbitrator leaves.

As for ombudspeople, for all their effectiveness they are not omniscient—and besides they tend to be overworked, unable to get to all the problems they would like to. Employee boards and work councils are limited by time delays and busy agenda.

But these are old problems that employees live with in any case. People were coping with them long before anyone thought of organizational rights. One gets in trouble with superiors for many reasons, and their displeasure over the exercise of a right would not be different from their irritation because of a personality conflict, a performance failure, or a disagreement over some workaday job routine. Constitutionalism would extend the risk, it would add to the possibilities of friction with senior employees, but at the same time it would add important satisfactions for bosses and subordinates alike.

NOTES

1. Richard E. Walton, "Improving the Quality of Work Life," *Harvard Business Review*, May-June 1974, p. 12.
2. *Christian Science Monitor,* February 27, 1975.
3. David W. Ewing, "Who Wants Employee Rights?" *Harvard Business Review*, November-December 1971, p. 22.
4. "California Products, Inc.," EA-A 257 (Harvard Business School, 1957).
5. Mark J. Thomas, "Employee Concern Review in the Corporation" (unpublished paper for the Mead Corporation), August 1975, Article II.
6. Thomas, Article III.
7. *New York Times,* November 2, 1975.
8. Dennis Chamot, "Professional Employees Turn to Unions," *Harvard Business Review*, May-June 1976, pp. 119–120.
9. See "Hull Manufacturing Company, E," ICH No. 4-675-213 (Harvard Business School, 1975).
10. *Wall Street Journal,* January 27, 1976.
11. Mack Hanan, "Make Way for the New Organization Man," *Harvard Business Review*, July-August 1971, p. 135.
12. Mary P. Rowe, "The Progress of Women in Educational Institutions" (unpublished paper, 1974).
13. Ewing, p. 155. A second survey was conducted in 1977.
14. This summary of experience at three English companies is based on J. Reynolds, "Employee Participation: a Trade Union View." In *Company Industrial Relations Policies,* edited by N. H. Cuthbert and K. H. Hawkins (London: Longman Group Ltd., 1973), pp. 148–154.

11

FROM "HOT LINES" TO COLD BALLOTS

There is another way of looking at the need for due process. Instead of adding a "judicial" mechanism to the organization, why not try to simplify the organization and bring employees closer to their bosses? This could be done by improving communications, so that unintentional errors and misunderstandings are reduced. It could also be done by giving aggrieved employees more power so that they can "make" top management listen.

The notion that injustices can be removed by improving communications is well-accepted. The theory is that an organization, like a biological system, is basically a system of relationships, and that good relationships depend on clear flows of information. If messages fail to get back and forth efficiently, the organization becomes sick. By the time the right people learn that something is wrong, the organizational body has a fever, a limp, or a missing limb (or, worse still, a request to appear before a Congressional committee).

Without question, many things that go wrong are due to faulty communications. How, then, are the faults to be removed?

An old answer is to remove the levels between operators and senior management—to reduce the "distance" between the top and bottom of the pyramid. In the long distance in between, policies become distorted, communications become garbled, feelings become lost. Middle-management bureaucrats become more interested in their own status and job security than in getting the work done. "Their bureaucratic manner is immense," intoned Chairman Mao Tsetung. "They beat their gongs to blaze the way. They cause people to become afraid just by looking at them."

So there has been a centuries-old dream of compressing the pyramid, of hacking out the layers in between, so that order-takers and order-givers can be brought closer together. This was one of the ideals motivating Fourierists, the "Bible Communists," and other so-called utopian societies of the nineteenth century.

Brook Farm, Robert Owen's "Villages of Cooperation," the Rappite villages, Icaria, Modern Times, Fruitland, and other such communities failed, partly because of their insistence on fighting the prevailing system. However, some of their ideals, including harmony through communications, have survived remarkably well, and today they find expression not as opposition to the economic system but as part of its administrative creed. For instance, a number of companies take pride in what they call "flat" organizations, meaning that middle-management staffs and groups have been cut to the bone. Indeed, the strenuous efforts to decentralize decision making in business and government spring partly from the conviction that the most direct way to better communications is to bring senders and receivers into closer proximity.

But poor communication is only one of many problems an organization may have; the structure must be shaped by other considerations, too, with the result that hierarchy and bureaucracy usually survive. Accordingly, some innovators have been casting around for means of reducing misunderstanding without altering the basic organizational scheme.

One promising innovation appears to be the "hot line." New England Telephone affords a good example.[1] New England's program of upward communications, called "Private

Lines," encourages and permits employees to ask responsible company officials about any matter of concern to them, from a problem with a supervisor to a troublesome organization policy. They can raise their questions by mail or by phone. They can remain anonymous if they desire. According to Bruce Harriman, until recently a vice-president of New England, thousands of questions have been handled in this relatively new program. Employees are making increasing use of phone calls instead of letters. Since the calls go to a full-time coordinating staff, the questioner can get a live answer and, equally important, amplify his or her question. Any time the coordinators are unable to handle a question, they refer it to an official who can.

According to company surveys, four employees in five are satisfied with the response they get to questions; more than nine in ten employees say they would use the system again. Some "Private Line" questions end up in a column of the company newspaper because of their potential wide interest. This column is the most widely read part of the publication.

But can a system like this do more than give employees a "warm feeling"? Also, what about the possibility that miscommunications are so inbred in human nature (including laziness in making enough effort to communicate) that structural changes and shortcuts may not really get to the heart of the difficulty?

Many people at New England Telephone are convinced that "Private Lines" is more than an anodyne. It has contributed to changes in training programs, work practices, working conditions, employee benefits, and career planning programs. On other occasions it has produced a valuable airing of difficult, sensitive problems. For instance, a white male manager anonymously complained about New England Telephone's affirmative action program for women and minority-group males, alleging that it cut down on the opportunities for promotion that men like himself had been counting on. A top executive replied, acknowledging that the competition for promotion had indeed increased. Both letters were strong and candid, and when published in the company newspaper they helped to get a difficult problem out in the open.

In a company or public organization, constitutionalism would be enhanced by a "hot line" system of this sort. An employee could call right away when he or she felt threatened as a consequence of "committing the truth" or doing some other act authorized in the organization's bill of rights.

Let us take our earlier example of the middle-aged engineer who was told to write substandard specifications for a new building or lose his job (Chapter 7). Chances are he is not going to disobey the order and get fired, for he is only a few years away from a vested pension and security in his old age. But if he can disobey the order *and stay on,* he will, for he feels strongly about his professional obligations. The "hot line" makes it possible for him to do that. He can call in, get in touch right away with a senior person, and tell his side of the story. So long as the company respects the right to conscience, and so long as the senior person is normally fair-minded, our engineer is going to be all right. It will be the boss who feels the heat.

The skeptic will ask, "But after the rogue boss is reprimanded and told to behave himself, what happens to our friend when, let us say, the two meet the next day?" Of course the boss is going to be sore. Of course he or she is going to be looking for some pretext to get even with the subordinate. But all this time the boss too is on probation, so to speak. If he starts nitpicking or sending the engineer on weird assignments, his motives will be suspect immediately. "He's trying to get even. He wasn't doing this sort of thing before."

At this point we must digress and turn briefly to organization theory. Social scientists have what is called a "theory of exit." In the American economy today, there is for many employees in many organizations a "high price of exit." This means it is difficult for an employee to quit when he or she is getting a raw deal. Unable readily to find an equally good job somewhere else, because of his circumstances or perhaps because of the employer's ability to blacklist him, he will be cautious indeed about using any threat of leaving in order to get his way in the organization. In short, he is not going to sound off or criticize; his voice is stilled. "If an organization has the ability to exact a high price for exit, it thereby acquires a powerful defense against one of the member's most potent weapons: the threat of exit. . . . [Such an organization] will often be able to repress both voice and exit."[2] The significance for organization theory is that the company or agency loses its capacity to respond. Failing to hear discontent, it becomes rigid and intolerant and does not wake up to the danger until it is too late.

This dangerous relationship can be broken by constitutionalism. In the "hot line" example of the engineer, the "high price of exit" is neutralized. The engineer does not have to decide between quitting or shutting up and doing what he is told. At only moderate risk, he can speak out *and* hold onto his job. Therefore, if it is true, as organization theorists believe, that a company or agency loses in the long run by suppressing employees' voices, constitutionalism would have salutary consequences for the economy and society.

Other companies have worked out different versions of the "hot line." One of the best-known is IBM's "Open Door." An employee who feels he or she is getting treated unfairly writes (after first trying to rectify the problem with the boss) to a senior executive of his or her choice—the next manager up the line, the head of the local organization, a vice-president, or the chief executive himself. The response is swift and personal. Also, IBM's policy is to take the employee viewpoint in such cases; that is, the senior person reads the complaint sympathetically, giving the employee the benefit of a doubt, at least until the situation is proved to be otherwise. There is no aversion to making the accused boss scuttle around and defend himself; the corporate attitude is that he is well enough paid to take a little insecurity.

"The Open Door is not exercised lightly," concludes IBM-watcher Nancy Foy. "Cases are investigated thoroughly and at each step the manager must be thoroughly prepared. Any manager who proposes to fire or demote an employee learns to anticipate an immediate Open Door unless he has taken exceptional precautions to avoid it."[3] In the corporate folklore there are many dramatic cases of "Open Door" use.

Since IBM already has a "bill of rights" on privacy (see Chapter 8), intrusions into an employee's private affairs or violations of the code concerning his file can be reported through the "Open Door." (They also can be reported anonymously through another system of written complaint called "Speak-Up!") Here is a company that has enacted constitutionalism in one area for its 160,000 employees in the United States.

In other organizations the upward communication-and-response systems work less swiftly and efficiently. Yet they may bring many injustices to light and protect as many rights as the organization wants to recognize. Here are some examples:

—At the Oscar Meyer Company, reports business journalist Lawrence Stessin, employees are invited to query management on any subject, and they receive either a personal reply or one which is printed in the employee newspaper.[4]

—Connecticut Mutual Life Insurance Company and American Airlines, as described in earlier chapters, also maintain systems for voicing employee complaints.

—Delta Air Lines (28,000 employees) holds periodic meetings at which employees are asked by top officials, after the supervisors and foremen are excused, "What's bothering you?" An employee does not have to reveal his or her identity—he can write the question on an unsigned card instead of standing up and asking. All questions are answered, either on the spot or in writing on a bulletin board after the meeting.[5]

In other systems, a senior executive—the personnel vice-president, for instance—is designated whose door is always open to employees who think they have been wronged; or a personnel manager investigates grievances and reports to a top executive; or an assistant to the president or vice-president looks into complaints. Judging from the *Harvard Business Review* survey, a majority of large companies have the first system, a near-majority the second system, and a small minority the third *can* work swimmingly. All to often, however, employees don't really believe the system works as it is supposed to, and so they think carefully before registering a complaint and testing their boss's good will. Indeed, many observers are frank to say that an unhappy employee has to be at wit's end in order to risk using the system.

THE POWER OF A COUNTERVAILING PRESENCE

As the economy becomes more technical, complicated, and "technology intensive," technical employees such as scientists and engineers find themselves in an enviable position. It is as if they were on one end of a teeter-totter with management, accountants, blue-collar workers, and all other nontechnical people at the other end. If the technicians jump off, the other end of the teeter-totter goes crashing down.

By nature, scientists and engineers are rights-conscious. Their professional competence and understanding grow from the free interchange of information. Open inquiry, questioning, and challenge are familiar ingredients of their approach to life.

Up to the mid- or early 1960s, however, employee rights received little attention in meetings of scientific societies. The annual conventions were a place to present papers on technical subjects and scout for jobs. Journals like *Science*, published by the American Association for the Advancement of Science, were repositories of comment on biological nitrogen fixation, postinhibitory rebound of neurons, and other exotic pursuits of scientism, undiluted by lay concerns.

During the Vietnam War and with the rise of environmental concerns, some scientists became political activists. At Bell Labs, an antiballistic missile contractor and the research and development arm of Western Electric, a group of scientists in the late 1960s publicly criticized Washington's policy on antiballistic missile development. A leading scientist at IBM openly criticized the United States' supersonic transport program.

Less publicized at the time, but of potentially greater importance in the long run, scientists and engineers began challenging management policies regarding employee rights. For instance, two West Coast organizations, Technical and Social Committee and Scientists and Engineers for Social and Political Action, put pressure on a major defense contractor to rehire an employee it had fired for publicly criticizing the company's minority hiring policies. On the East Coast, an organization called Computer Professionals for Peace, formed originally to protest the Vietnam War, branched into the invasion of privacy question.

In 1972 a small band of Atomic Energy Commission safety researchers appeared in public hearings to question the adequacy of emergency cooling equipment being used in new atomic power reactors. Other scientists in industry and government have covertly supplied the Union of Concerned Scientists, newspaper reporters, and other critics with information embarrassing to top policy makers. Still others—for instance, three General Electric engineers and a Federal Nuclear Regulatory Commission engineer who were worried about nuclear power safeguards in 1976— have resigned in order to campaign for their convictions.

Science magazine reflects the significant change in scientists' concerns. After Louis V. McIntire, a chemical engineer, was sacked by Du Pont for writing a satirical novel (see Chapter 6), *Science* ran a two-page spread describing his legal case and the various organized efforts to protect scientist-employee rights. Current issues of *Science* touch repeatedly on questions of professional rights, obligations, and ethics.

In the spring of 1975, the Committee on Scientific Freedom and Responsibility of the American Association for the Advancement of Science issued a report urging scientists and engineers to blow the whistle on their employers when they saw their work being used for morally dubious ends. The Committee also urged scientific societies to defend members who were persecuted for protesting an employer's policy. Such members should be staked to the costs of fighting their employers in court on such questions, the Committee said.

Can scientific and engineering societies actually change the long-established habits of large and powerful organizations? They do not call strikes, as a union does. They do not have paid lobbyists in Washington and the state capitals. Nor do they have "hot lines" to the board room or chief executive's office. Besides, power politics has never seemed to be the strong suit of the scientific mind. Perhaps it was for one or a combination of these reasons that the California Society of Professional Engineers failed to back effectively the three outspoken engineers who were fired by San Francisco's Bay Area Rapid Transit system (see Chapter 6). The Society gave the engineers moral support only—not enough to force the employer agency to give the jobs back or compensate the men financially.

Yet, judging from the example set by the American Chemical Society, professional groups can be potent. The ACS has never boycotted or picketed an employer, least of all threatened to explode a laboratory or irradiate a board room. Yet by virtue of the *presence* of its countervailing power, it seems to have bent many an organization to its view of fairness.

The ACS makes its position known in various ways. It publishes a pamphlet called *Guidelines for Employers* (most recently revised in 1974) which sets forth such rules as that chemist employees should be free to participate in political and community activities of their choice and that a chemist with ten or more years of service in the organization should not be fired except for cause and after review of the case by at least two levels of senior management. The *Guidelines* proscribe blacklisting.

The ACS also has set up a legal fund to lend chemists and chemical engineers the necessary fees for going to court and contesting poor employer treatment. It comes to the aid of members who request assistance in dealing with employer abuse; it investigates the situation and, if the member chemist does indeed seem to have been fouled, it seeks to remedy the problem by suasion—"by discussions and through correspondence," in the words of its official memorandum to members. It may use consultants for this purpose. Not always does it take the chemist-employee's side; it may decide that the organization treated him fairly.

The nearest the ACS ever comes to blows with an employer is citing the employer by name in its publication, *Chemical and Engineering News.* This is done in an inconspicuous column, and sometimes even in small print. Yet the citations receive swift and wide attention—only the most callous employer is indifferent to them. For instance, the ACS cited Pennwalt's pharmaceutical division in Rochester, New York for "unprofessional termination" of several chemists; it cited Royal Oak Charcoal Co. for "treating an ACS member in an unacceptable manner and for failure to cooperate with ACS in investigating the matter."

Indicative of the quiet but effective power of the ACS is its growing case load. In the mid-1960s only three appeals from members were under consideration; by the mid-1970s, six times as many cases of maltreatment were under consideration.

For the scientist or engineer who is being drawn and quartered here and now—in real time, as technicians say—it may be insufficient comfort that a professional society, proceeding indirectly with factual investigation and moral persuasion, will exert pressure on an offending employer six months from now. On the other hand, the presence and stature of professional societies is such that, once they take a firm and clear position, the *responsive* employer may take action without further pressure.

Some ACS leaders want to amend the National Labor Relations Act to include standards like those in the *Guidelines* and make them applicable to all professional and white-collar employees. Alan C. Nixon, then president of the organization, put the proposal in writing to a top-level committee in 1973. While this development may be some time in coming, it tells us something about the seriousness of the ACS approach.

What about that other form of countervailing power, managerial associations and unions? Most Americans probably do not know there are such unions, but Emanuel Kay, a management consultant, reports the birth of one in 1973.

It happened in a public transit authority in the Northeast, Kay writes, and in most ways it looked like any other union representation election. There was a representative of the state labor commission, a representative from management, and an attorney for the petitioning union. Appointed people counted the ballots, verified the numbers, and set aside challenged ballots. As the counting went on, there was "a fairly monotonous cadence of yes . . . yes . . . yes, interrupted by an occasional no. It very quickly became apparent that the petitioners would win, and they did. There was a smattering of applause and handshakes around, and the winners went off to celebrate a four-year legal and administrative effort to establish their union."[6] However, the ballots had been cast not by assembly workers, mechanics, or drivers but by middle managers in the company, and the union thus formed was a middle-management organization, not a new branch of the AFL-CIO or Teamsters.

At one time some people held high hopes for managerial unions. Particularly at the cavernous reaches of the middle management level, there was darkening discontent with rightlessness and maltreatment from top management. Unfortunately for proponents, a group of twenty-five managers in the purchasing and procurement department of Bell Aerospace Company in 1974 lost their bid to win collective bargaining rights under the National Labor Relations Act. The U.S. Supreme Court, in a five-to-four decision, ruled that managerial employees are not covered by the Act.

This decision temporarily halted the managerial union movement. In one form or another, however, it is likely to appear in the future. Middle managers and supervisors keep complaining about "mushroom management," by which they mean that, just as mushrooms are grown in cool dark caves in rich nitrogenous soil and harvested when they grow to size, so middle managers are kept in the dark, covered with manure, and canned as soon as they stick their heads up.

Associations at the middle management level could be a potent force to ensure due process and other rights. Not only could they do for the millions of people at this level what trade unions and professional associations do for their members, but because of their strategic position in business and public organizations they could help to assure rights for other employees as well.

However, no light is visible yet at the end of this tunnel. Kay describes one incident which suggests the latent hostility of many leaders to middle management organizations. In one venerable manufacturing concern, the middle managers got together and as a group asked top management to realign their salaries with those of blue-collar workers. Abruptly and with little explanation, top management turned them down. So the middle managers formed an association and pressed harder for their proposals. The top men refused to deal with them. In desperation, they set up a picket line. "Top management responded by firing the leaders and giving the remaining middle managers one hour to get back to work—which they did."[7]

In the public sector, employees can turn for help to the National Federation of Federal Employees. It has been a growing power behind employee rights.

COULD DUE PROCESS BE A BALLOT?

At a recent stockholder meeting of a large corporation, a man stood up, waved insistently for the chairman's attention, and was finally recognized. He launched into an angry criticism of the company's ethics in obtaining contracts. What was unusual about this scene was not the man's tirade—other stockholders were critical, too—but his status. He was an employee of the company as well as a shareholder. Had he been an employee only, he would not have had a meeting place in which to speak out.

Possibly the man found a pink slip on his desk when he returned to the workplace—I don't know. Probably he did not, however, for reportedly he had taken top management to task in previous annual meetings. In all likelihood there was at least one boss who wanted to fire him. But one can imagine other managers shaking their heads. "It would give us a black eye to fire an employee who is also a stockholder." Perhaps another voice chimed in: "After all, isn't this company owned by and operated *for* the shareholders?"

There are all sorts of reasons that employee stock voting is no panacea to the problems of protecting employee rights. Yet in this simple procedure there is a potent tool for some situations. If many employees were shareholders, they would loom as a constant threat to the boss or management group that sought to deprive an employee of his or her rights—simply by virtue of their being able to "make a stink" in front of the board chairman and reporters at the next stockholder meeting, or before then in a letter to stockholders.

What is more, an employee-shareholder group might be able to sway other shareholders to vote a change in top management. Indeed, employee-shareholder power has already proved itself, although not for the purpose of corporate constitutionalism. During the 1960s, three employees of a Connecticut company, Terry Steam Turbine Company, purchased one share each of stock in the firm. Then they requested permission to inspect the shareholder list. They wanted to tell the shareholders, prior to the forthcoming annual shareholder meeting, about some labor relations problems. (The employees had a particular interest in this because they were also members of the union negotiating committee.) Management denied their request. Though the corporation law for Connecticut gave shareholders the right to inspect the list "for any proper purpose," management insisted that the men's motives were improper. They sought to help the union's cause, not the company's, said management. The shareholder-employees took the company to court and won. The court did not feel that their affiliation with the union necessarily inspired them to oppose the company's or shareholders' interests.[8]

It would seem, therefore, that the law is no barrier to the employee who would buy a share of stock in order to get the address list of all shareholders and send them a letter about an employee rights problem. Of course, this employee can also attend shareholder meetings and speak his or her piece there, as was done in the example cited. In many cases it would not be necessary for the dissident group to persuade a majority of the stockholders to vote for a policy correction. It would be enough to present their case cogently and produce a wave of sympathy.

If many employees in a company were to buy one share of stock apiece, might they then become a strong voting block at a shareholder meeting? One might think so at first, in view of the numerous companies employing a thousand or more employees. In actuality, however, such an employee voting block would compare with North Dakota's electoral vote in the presidential electoral college—it would scarcely count. To pick at random a sizable company, suppose each of the Mead Corporation's 27,000 employees were to buy one share and show up at the annual meeting. There are 15.1 million shares in that corporation, each with one vote. Therefore the employee voting block at Mead would represent less than two-tenths of 1 percent of the votes. To buy a bare majority of the shares at the price of $17 quoted late in

1976, the employees would have to invest more than $128,350,000, or about $4,750 each.

RCA's 116,000 employees, an impressive number, would have even less clout with one share each at a shareholder meeting—they would have 1.5 tenths of 1 percent of the votes. To buy a bare majority of the shares at the late 1976 price of $25, they would have to invest nearly $933,000,000, or more than $8,000 each. In a larger corporation like General Motors, the problem would be more difficult still.

As things stand, therefore, employee-shareholders would be a voice at an annual meeting—a voice that probably would be listened to—but they would be negligible as a voting power. Only if the law were changed to give each *shareholder* one vote could an employee voting block become powerful.

Americans are so accustomed to the "one share, one vote" rule for corporations that they are shocked by any suggestion that the voting might be done differently. After all, doesn't the owner who has a large sum invested deserve more votes than the owner with a piddling investment? The logic is irrefutable so long as we want to measure a stockholder's influence by the money he puts up, as we do at poker and other games. But if we were to adopt more egalitarian values, saying (as we do at political elections) that the *person* is the most important thing, regardless of his property interests, then a "one shareholder, one vote" rule might make a great deal of sense—or, as a compromise, a rule limiting any one shareholder to a maximum of ten, twenty, or some other small number of votes.

A law professor at Cornell, David L. Ratner, has made a detailed and knowledgeable case for limiting shareholders to one or a few votes.[9] There seems little reason to believe that his proposal will get far in today's climate. But with a shift in just a few assumptions about what is equitable—and such a shift could indeed occur with public opinion about business as volatile as it is—Ratner's arguments would be persuasive.

Not all countries follow the U.S. rule of a vote per share,

as Ratner points out. For instance, Uruguay limits a stockholder to six votes, no matter how many shares he or she owns; and in Sweden, Switzerland, and other European countries the articles of incorporation may limit the number of votes any shareholder may cast. In Germany, when the Volkswagen Company was opened to public ownership, a law was passed limiting any one stockholder to the votes that would accrue from owning one ten-thousandth of the shares.

Perhaps more important to many Americans, our own early corporations limited shareholder voting power. William Penn's Free Society of Traders in Pennsylvania, chartered in England in 1682, limited a Pennsylvanian owning 1,000 or more acres of inhabited land in the province to three votes for six or more shares, two votes for two shares, and one vote for one share.[10]

According to Ratner, more than 300 private business corporations were chartered in the United States between the Revolution and 1801. The majority of these companies were "quasi-public," such as transportation or water firms. In most of the charters, a stockholder's voting power was limited to twenty, ten, or a lesser number of votes. The great federalist, Alexander Hamilton, argued for such a rule. Restrictions on voting power were popular because of widespread public concern that powerful property interests could weaken democratic government.

If a one-vote-per-shareholder limit went into effect today, employees in most sizable companies could, by acquiring one share per employee, become a strong voting block. For example, if only half of IBM's U.S. employees voted together, they would cast about 13 percent of the votes—a force to be reckoned with. In 1969, according to Ratner's computations, the employees of General Motors, if each invested $65 to buy a share, would have acquired more than one-third of the votes.

Even if adopted, this revolutionary approach would not guarantee constitutionalism. Not all employees could be expected to agree on violations of employee rights; in the absence of strong leadership from a union or professional association, employee opinion might be so apathetic or divided that a despotic management could go its way unhindered. Moreover, not all employees could be expected to buy a share, so as to be entitled to a vote.

But employees may have an ace in the hole. It is the Employee Stock Ownership Plan with the tax advantages signed into law in the Tax Reform Act of 1976. Louis Kelso, U.S. Senator Russell Long, and others who worked long and hard for the ESOP principle were not thinking of employee rights as the gain to be achieved. They were thinking of motivation. In their view, ESOPs were a way to motivate employees to believe in capitalism and reject socialism. What is happening in a growing number of companies, however, is that ESOPs also give employees a potent means of control. This may not have been the objective of ESOP promoters, but in time it is going to be a result of enormous importance.

As this is written, only a short time has elapsed since ESOPs were recognized and given favored treatment in the tax law. Yet already in hundreds of companies employees have gained enough voting power to bend corporate policy when they want to do so. Though not able to dominate, they can influence—they can demand and get attention. Let the winds of constitutionalism blow just a little harder in the corporate world, fanning the desire for firmer employee rights, and almost certainly we will see the employee-shareholder capturing a prominent role in many companies.

OTHER APPROACHES THAT WORK

Within an organization there are still other ways to enforce an employee bill of rights and assure constitutionalism. While they may lack the broad promise of "hot lines" and countervailing power groups, they could be useful to some people in some situations and are worth noting here.

Employment contracts. When executives and key professionals negotiate with an employer, they may try to put in writing a statement of mutual obligations and responsibilities. Such contracts rarely can keep an employer from getting rid of an employee who is found offensive, as both chief executives (for example, Semon Knudsen, fired as president of Ford Motor Company with five years still to run on his contract) and scientists have discovered. On the other hand, if they provide for payments to the employee in case of discharge, they serve both as a financial shelter for the ex-worker and as a financial deterrent to the employer. Thus they increase the possibilities that rights will be asserted and that they will be tolerated.

Employment contracts have built-in limitations. The agreements must be in accordance with state law; it must be clear that the parties are authorized to make a contract; the length of time to be covered must be reasonable; and the language must be clear enough to avoid varying interpretations.

The American Chemical Society and other professional associations have encouraged scientists and engineers to make employment contracts. Top executives often negotiate them with prospective employers. So far, the rights mentioned in this book have not been incorporated in such contracts, but they could be.

Directors representing employees. In theory, the board of directors or trustees could be the body that polices management and assures constitutionalism. Especially in other countries, support has grown for the notion that at least some members of the board should be elected by employees. These employee representatives could look after the interests of people on the payroll just as other board members have traditionally represented the owners. A leading British magazine states:

> Giving the employees the vote [by representation on the board] would not just tidy up a theoretical nonsense. It might provide the sort of stimulus to directorial efforts which the shareholders on their own fail to give. The directors would have to present the annual results to the employees just as

much as to shareholders, but probably with less chance of
pulling the wool over their eyes. It was significant in the case
of one . . . flop, for example, that large numbers of very able
employees, who quickly found out what a muddle the group's
affairs were getting into, were fired as soon as they made protest. If the employees had had the right to raise these matters
at an annual general meeting, the shareholders might well
never have allowed the situation to continue as it did.[11]

In West Germany, where employee representation is required by law, and Sweden, where leading companies like
Volvo have experimented with the approach, the directors
elected by workers pay much attention to working conditions, work relationships, "job enrichment," and other
quality-of-work-life matters as well as things like pay rates
and pensions. If a company had a bill of rights, its enforcement would be one of the key responsibilities for an
employee-elected director.

In the United States there is great opposition to this approach. For one thing, could one or a few employee directors or trustees keep track of what is going on in a sizable
organization with scores of plants, offices, or agencies lo-
cated in many regions? A director in New York can monitor
the financial performance of a plant in New Mexico, if there
is a good financial reporting system, but what about
monitoring such a subtle matter as employee rights?

For another thing, U.S. management authorities usually
object to turning the board into a collection of special interest representatives. Traditionally, directors and trustees
have been appointed to guard the interests of the organization as a whole. They may have widely varying vantage
points and skills, but the growth and prosperity of the *enterprise* is the common object of concern. If this tradition is
reversed, with directors elected to look after certain con-
stituencies, the board becomes more a political institution
than a management agency. This could be a step backwards.

Instead of having employees elect one or a few representatives, why not assign certain members of the board to "au-
dit" constitutionalism in the organization, much as financial

committees of the board concentrate on money matters and planning committees focus on major investments? Where there are exceptionally able directors or trustees, this approach could accomplish something—and even where there are not, it would be useful. However, the typical director is not able to delve deeply into operations. Especially with the trend to the so-called "outside board," that is, the board made up of people from outside the organization, rather than the organization's own managers, it is all a director can do to keep up with the heavy dockets, replete with data, that await him or her at the quarterly or semiannual meeting.

Although the board of directors or trustees could be very helpful, in the organizations where constitutionalism is most needed, top management is least likely to organize a strong board—and it is top management that decides who will serve, at least until a court steps in. In the Penn Central disaster, the fiasco at Mattel, and many other cases of corporate misfortune cited earlier in this book, the board was not policing management, it was in bed with management. Some cynical observers have come to believe, as a result of such incidents, that the board is worse than nothing, for it creates the illusion that someone is there on top who knows what is going on and has the gumption to correct errors when in fact the resident boards of directors are passive and often uninformed.

"Industrial democracy." Some U.S. companies have been experimenting with ways of getting employees to do more of the decision making. In these organizations employees have both direct and indirect power to discipline offenders against employee rights.

Among smaller companies, Donnelly Mirrors is a leading example of industrial democracy in action. This unusual firm in Holland, Michigan manages to draw workers into many of the most important problems to be solved. For instance, in 1970 management was considering proposals to place all employees on salary (many had been piece-rate workers), to remove time clocks, and to adopt some new standards for giving pay increases. Instead of management's deciding what was best, it asked the workers—the governed, so the speak—to vote on the proposals.[12] In numerous other ways Donnelly encourages such a spirit of participation.

In the world of big business, Procter and Gamble is a leading experimenter. In the late 1960s it started a new plant in Lima, Ohio. According to Charles Krone, the head of organizational development at P&G headquarters, this plant "was designed from the ground up to be democratic." For instance, conference rooms and labs were put next to the production area so that workers, supervisors, and researchers could get together quickly and work out a problem. Hiring and firing has been done by worker teams. Employees do not allow one another to become very specialized—they want every person to be able to handle different jobs. "The outstanding characteristic of the P&G approach," sums up David Jenkins, not ordinarily an admirer of corporate management, "is its insistence on a truly 'open' attitude."[13]

Few if any government organizations have taken steps in the direction of employee democracy. One public agency executive dismissed "industrial democracy" contemptuously as an idealistic experiment that could work only in the higher latitudes of Sweden and Norway. It was "honey from the icebox (cold sweets don't spread)."

One may wonder if an organization that has succeeded in becoming "open" needs a bill of rights for employees. It may already be attaining the rewarding human objective that a bill of rights is designed to help bring about. Perhaps the real question is: Will management stay so enlightened? When the team at the top changes some day, as it must, the new heads are under no commitment to keep things as they were, in the absence of formal provisions for constitutionalism.

NOTES

1. See Bruce Harriman, "Up and Down the Communications Ladder," *Harvard Business Review*, September-October 1974, p. 143.
2. Albert O. Hirschman, *Exit, Voice, and Loyalty* (Cambridge, Mass.: Harvard University Press, 1970), pp. 96–97.
3. Nancy Foy, *The Sun Never Sets on IBM* (New York: Morrow, 1974), p. 126.
4. *New York Times,* November 17, 1974.
5. *New York Times,* April 28, 1974.
6. Emanuel Kay, *The Crisis in Middle Management* (New York: Amacom, American Management Association, 1974), p. 42.
7. Kay, p. 50.
8. *De Rosa* v. *Terry Steam Turbine Co.,* 214 A. 2d 684 (1965).
9. See David L. Ratner, "The Government of Business Corporations: Critical Reflections on the Rule of 'One Share, One Vote,'" *Cornell Law Review,* November 1970, p. 1.
10. Ratner, p. 5.
11. "The Ugly Mug of Capitalism," *Management Today,* January 1974, p. 93.
12. "Donnelly Mirrors, Inc.," ICH No. 2-473-088 (Harvard Business School, 1973).
13. David Jenkins, *Job Power* (New York: Doubleday & Company, Inc., 1973), p. 235.

12

POTENT REMEDIES IN COURTROOMS AND LEGISLATURES

Ideally, it should never be necessary for employees to go outside the company or public agency for help when their rights are invaded. Turning to mechanisms within the organization, they should be able to get their grievances handled fairly. But suppose the organization is shot through and through with injustices? Suppose that it was born crooked? Or suppose the wronged employee is one of those unhappy types who rubs everyone the wrong way and so antagonizes the arbitrator, ombudsperson, "hot line" official, or whatever other person might help him or her that justice is not done in the usual way?

When rights cannot be protected by procedures within the organization, employees should be able to go outside. Here is where the courts, administrative tribunals, and state and federal legislatures come in. There is much they can do. There is much that employees who feel wronged are now asking them to do. It used to be that salaried employees, who traditionally have not belonged to unions, departed as quickly and quietly as possible when the boss no longer wanted their services. No more. Company after company can attest to the willingness of discharged employees to fight their eviction in court. In 1974, Standard Oil Company of California paid about $2 million in back wages to 140 discharged sales department workers who charged they were forced out because of age. Other companies have had similar experiences. Public agencies, too, have been taken to court.

When due process is not or cannot be forthcoming in an organization, the atmosphere can become poisonous for the dissident employee, even though there may be policies that protect him or her from immediate discharge (such as a "tenure" rule because of years of past service). As we have seen, the dissident may be cut off from a suitable place to work, supplies, and other assistance. He may be isolated or transferred to the boondocks. He may be ordered to take psychiatric tests, to fill out needless forms and applications over and over again, to write reports on stupid subjects. The miasma may become unbearable.

Those who have witnessed such treatment sometimes remark on the efficiency with which all members of the department seem to cooperate, perhaps because of their own fear of retaliation if they don't. The employee who at first insisted he would never resign finds himself unable to take it anymore, and finally bolts for the door.

Until recently, that would be the end of the story. But the situation is changing. Judges, lawmakers, and other outsiders may now come to the aid of the beleaguered employee.

Because legal remedies are costly for the organization as well as for society at large, they ought to be made the course of last resort. According to a personnel official in a tire company, in 1975 it cost up to $20,000 for the firm to fight a contested discharge in court. Sooner or later, such costs have to be passed on to the consumer or taxpayer.

Moreover, in an outside legal forum, away from the scene of action and personnel involved, proof may be difficult to produce. Also, quite some time may elapse before a decision is reached. (George B. Geary, the U.S. Steel salesman who criticized management, waited seven years for a final decision by Pennsylvania's Supreme Court.) Facing idleness and poverty for months or years on end, the suing employee could become a basket case before his or her docket number is turned up.

HANDLING CASES OF ABUSIVE DISCHARGE

For the sake of brevity, I shall borrow from Lawrence E. Blades the term "abusive discharge," using it to refer to cases where employees are fired for standing on their rights (and where poor performance by the employee or a forced cutback of the staff are not plausible explanations of the discharge).

When a competent employee with years of service is fired for refusing to submit to a boss's improper or overreaching demands, the boss feels guilt in a way not experienced when firing an employee for incompetence or laziness. Therefore the firing is apt to be malicious. For the luckless employee, the cost of dismissal can be staggering. He or she may have to go through months and possibly years without regular earnings, and face the humiliation of being avoided by former associates.

Because of the high financial and psychological costs of losing his job, an abusively discharged employee should be able to sue for damages. "If the employee had some assurance that he would not have to bear such losses, he would be in a far better position to withstand oppression at the hands of his employer," states Blades.[1] His exegesis of the law and recommendations are the basis of many points in this section.

There are good precedents for letting the ex-employee sue for damages. For instance, if a person is discharged unlawfully for engaging in labor union activities, the National Labor Relations Board can grant him or her both reinstatement and damages in the form of back pay. Also, a victim of discrimination because of race, sex, or age can collect compensation for working time lost. On the other hand, most of the abusively discharged persons mentioned in earlier chapters were not compensated for their unemployment—or, if they were, received only token damages (Holodnak is an example). Something is askew in society when we compensate an employee who is discriminated against for race, sex, or union involvement but not the employee penalized for resisting or criticizing unethical management behavior.

What would be the legal basis for collecting damages? Except for employees who have written employment contracts that cover the problem, the law of torts, not the law of contract, provides the needed umbrella. The ex-employee who sues for damages on the basis of an unwritten, implied employment contract is up against heavy odds. But "the more elastic principles of tort law," as Blades calls them, are applicable. Tort law is the basis for many of our damage suits where we claim bodily injury, mental anguish, or other harm due to the defendant's improper actions and ulterior motives. (Contract law, by contrast, applies to cases where a person defaults on written or implied obligations—for instance, a builder who puts the shingles on upside down.)

Should the employee be reinstated in the old job? In many cases, yes—but not always. Sometimes there is no way an abusively discharged employee can find happiness again with the old employer. The very sight of him or her may produce guilt and remorse among supervisors and co-workers. Yet this normally would be the solution under the law of contract. Tort law offers a more flexible answer. Under tort law, reinstatement could be considered, but if it were apparent that this would be unwise, the court or tribunal could specify other forms of compensation.

How great should the damages be? At the minimum, they should cover the wages, salaries, bonuses, and fringe benefits the ex-employee would normally have received—and could expect to receive in the future—if he or she had not been discharged. (Naturally, the ex-employee is expected to seek a new job diligently, and once he starts getting paid again, the old employer is off the hook.)

But, as Blades points out, "Deterrence should also be a prime objective of the remedy for abusive discharge."[2] Therefore the ex-employee should also be able to claim damages to compensate him for being the victim of a wrongful act. Punitive damages are collectible in tort actions, though usually not in actions for breach of contract. "Punitive damages are absolutely necessary to impress upon the people in authority that an employee's constitutional rights cannot be infringed," stated New Jersey Superior Court

Judge Merritt Lane, Jr., in the recent case of Patricia Endress. She was awarded damages of $104,000 and was returned to her job as a student adviser at Brookdale Community College after being fired for writing an editorial criticizing the school board chairman.[3]

How is the ex-employee to prove abusive discharge? The burden should be on him or her to offer clear and convincing evidence. It should *not* be up to the employer to prove that the discharge was for incompetence, laziness, or economic reasons. If the burden of proof is on the employer, managers will be inhibited from building the most able and efficient staffs they can.

When the company, public agency, university, or other employer is taken to court, therefore, it should not even have to defend itself unless the ex-employee can present facts and witnesses indicating that he was discharged for exercising an accepted right of speech, privacy, or conscience. In the absence of such evidence at the outset, the case should be thrown out.

If the ex-employee does have such evidence, the employer can defend himself in various ways. Calling his own witnesses, he can show that the claim is spurious. Also, if from time to time the boss made specific notations about the plaintiff's failures on the job (and if, best of all, the boss talked frankly to the employee about the failures), those records can be offered in evidence. Many well-managed organizations make such records as a matter of course. They would not have to do anything new because of employee rights.

The longer the ex-employee was on the job, the better his or her case. This is one reason that the chairman of Xerox Corporation insists on personally reviewing discharges of employees who have served eight or more years.[4] If management was doing its job, such employees must have been working competently or they would not have stayed on the payroll all that time. If management was not doing its job, and allowing incompetents to stay on the payroll, the sooner it becomes aware of the situation, the better.

If the ex-employee can point to several years of service and such indicators of good work as regular or special pay raises, improvements in title and responsibility, commendations from the employer, and/or witnesses to his or her good work—as well as, of course, facts indicating that the discharge (or demotion or humiliating transfer) was abusive—the employer is going to have a rough time.

DEFINING THE LAW OF ABUSIVE DISCHARGE

The law of abusive discharge is yet to be defined. There are various possibilities.

First, it could be defined by the courts. Deciding on a case-by-case basis, as the federal courts have started to do for public employees in the *Pickering* line of cases, the courts might gradually build a common law of abusive discharge. However, this might take years, and in the meantime there would be great uncertainty, which would discourage victims of abusive discharge from defending their rights.

Second, statutes covering abusive discharge could be enacted by the states. Statutes have important advantages. They are, or should be, clear and definitive. Also, they could specify that the discharged employee could sue for damages (which might not be the case if the question were left to common law). However, state legislation may be halting and uneven, with certain rights created in some states but not in others, and some states acting aggressively but others not at all. This means that quite a few employees are going to be left out.

Therefore federal legislation is the best method. It would apply equally to all companies engaged in interstate commerce, all concerns interested in federal contracts, and all agencies of the federal government. Federal statutes make the courts' job easier. In the opinion of Blades, "the courts could be left to perform the function, for which they are well suited, of giving reasoned elaboration to a broad statutory provision. And through a process of continuing judicial articulation a detailed bill of rights for all employees could be provided."[5]

Senator Edward M. Kennedy's proposed Federal Employees Disclosure Act of 1975 (S. 1210), though a very truncated version of the legislation we propose here, suggests the kind of concreteness and definitiveness that Congress can give. The bill sets forth the right; that is, it authorizes federal employees to make disclosures of certain kinds of information that are in the public interest. It then tells them how to act: They can bring a civil action in a federal district court, and the court is authorized to provide complete relief—restraining orders, interlocutory injunctions to prevent the threatened violation, reinstatement, damages, whatever is needed. If the complaining employee wins, he or she is entitled under the bill to reasonable attorney fees and other costs. Certain questions of proof also are clarified.

The same approach could be taken in the legislation proposed here, although it would apply to corporate as well as to governmental employees, and specify more rights. Only employees of state and city governments, and employees of firms not interested in doing business with the federal government and not engaged in interstate commerce, would be beyond the reach of Congress. Presumably, Congress also would exempt smaller companies, say, those with fewer than fifty employees.

If employee constitutionalism is a good thing for federal employees and for companies subject to some federal control, some people will argue, it should also be a good thing for state government employees, companies not beholden to Washington, and organizations such as universities, arts institutes, and community welfare agencies. Therefore would not a constitutional amendment be a more fitting approach? An amendment would apply to all employees except those who might be specifically excepted, such as workers in small firms and professional partnerships. I shall defer further discussion of a constitutional amendment to the final chapter.

FEDERAL CHARTERING OF CORPORATIONS

If Congress wanted to cover only business employers, it could take another route: federal chartering of corporations. The notion of federal chartering makes most business leaders uneasy. Also it is anathema to legislators alarmed at the spread of big government.

Nevertheless, there is a certain logic in favor of federal chartering. It would be a way to even out the enormous discrepancies and inconsistencies in state corporation laws. Also, it would be a way of recognizing that much business affects the broad public interest. Some leading economists support this view. John Kenneth Galbraith, at a Senate hearing in 1971, stated that the giant corporation "must be regarded by any man with a reasonably unfettered mind as a public institution." Willard F. Mueller said, "It is appropriate that large corporations be treated and recognized as quasipublic institutions." Walter Adams, describing the social consequences of many managerial decisions, concluded that "they can hardly claim immunity from public scrutiny and public accountability."[6] If views like these are accepted, federal chartering is an alternative worth pondering.

Moreover, this route has some advantages from the corporate standpoint. To qualify for a federal charter, a company might be required to guarantee its employees only a bill of rights that meets certain general requirements. The precise scope and wording of the bill could be adapted to fit the special circumstances of the company. For example, retailers employing many part-time clerks and normally experiencing high turnover could write into their bills of rights different guarantees of privacy, let us say, from what would be appropriate for large manufacturers employing mostly full-time employees with low turnover. Thus, IBM, as we have seen, collects a sparse legal history on applicants for employment. More information may be unfairly prejudicial, IBM's management believes. But for a supermarket such a sparse record of run-ins with the law conceivably might handicap management; it might be fairer all around to solicit more information from the applicant, and perhaps also

do more checking of statements supplied than IBM does
(IBM prefers not to hire outside agencies to verify applicants' statements but to make any desired confirmations
itself).

WHERE SHOULD ABUSIVE DISCHARGE
CASES BE HEARD?

Who should hear cases of abusive discharge? Blades feels
that civil rights tribunals and fair employment practices
commissions might be better than the courts. The Iowa law
dean argues:

> This approach would provide the advantages of administra-
> tive responsibility and expertise in a limited area, for the task
> of such a commission in determining the employer's motive
> would be essentially the same in cases of abusive discharge as
> in cases where discrimination is claimed. Also, the range of
> remedies available to such commissions is typically wider
> than that at the disposal of the courts. . . .[7]

If administrative tribunals heard cases first, the federal
district or appeals courts would hear only appeals (as they
do when a decision of, say, an unemployment commission or
the Internal Revenue Service is appealed). Thus the courts
could set broad guidelines for the tribunals, but they would
not be deluged with hundreds of cases, lengthening their
already long backlogs.

Moreover, some observers are coming to the conclusion
that many disputes can be handled better outside the court-
room. The adversary proceedings that characterize court-
room cases are unnecessary to accomplish justice in
numerous types of cases, especially those involving modest
claims and simple types of evidence. "We need to develop
procedures to fit the crime, to fit the tort, to fit the particular
problem, rather than using courts as all-purpose problem
solvers," states Thomas Ehrlich, former dean of the Stanford

Law School and now president of Legal Services Corporation.[8] He cites the proposal of Federal judge Shirley Hufstedler of California that "economy courts" be established. In these courts, lawyers would be permitted to represent clients but the emphasis would be on oral presentations, with depositions, charts, letters, and other paper filings kept to a minimum. "Economy courts" might also be the right place for routine types of employee rights cases.

A good example of the kind of case that probably should not go to the regular courts is that of the transferred Boston firefighters. Three men, with more than thirty years of service between them in the Boston Fire Department, testified in 1975 that they were put under official pressure to contribute to Boston mayor Kevin White's political campaign. They protested; their story got publicized. They were then transferred from their choice positions on the arson squad to less desirable tasks. The firefighters claimed the transfers were retaliation for their speaking out in the public interest. Their superiors got hot under the collar. A city official insisted the move was a "budget cutback, not a retaliation." The case is being fought out in court. Is it really necessary to sort out the facts of such a dispute in mountains of documentation, legal ratiocination, and testimony sieved through the traditional rules of judicial evidence? A simple, more flexible, less formal hearing before a qualified administrative tribunal or "economy court" should be able to do the job more efficiently.

THE PUBLIC INTEREST LAWYER

Who is likely to take the case, in a regular or special court, of the employee who alleges abusive discharge or other forms of employer retaliation? Many good attorneys find it more rewarding to handle the problems of a sizable corporation or government agency than of an unemployed engineer or sales manager with $1,800 in the bank.

The public interest lawyer could be the answer. Prominent since the late 1960s, public interest lawyers deal with issues whose outcome will affect the welfare of many people as well as the interests of the plaintiff in a given case. Well-known examples of public interest law are suits brought by groups of citizens to stop air pollution, or the suit that a mother brings to force television stations to offer more balanced programs for children. Cases of abusive discharge qualify as public interest law because the working lives of many other employees are affected by the findings.

In typical cases of public interest law, the plaintiffs do not seek damages. For example, in the television programming case, the mother seeks only to have the network upgrade its programming for the sake of her children. In this respect the abusively discharged employee is different because he or she does claim damages (at least, if the counsel of earlier pages is followed). Though such restitution may take the case out of the category of strict public interest law, one result could be that ex-employees might find it easier to locate capable attorneys to represent them.

The public interest bar, as the roster of attorneys interested in these cases is called, does not have many bartenders. In 1974 it was estimated that only 100 or so public interest lawyers could be found, and even they were concentrated in a few major cities.[9] Most of these attorneys have been subsidized by grants from foundations, such as the National Wildlife Federation and Common Cause, by independent family incomes, or by collections; of course, many are motivated by fierce desires to serve a worthy cause. This new branch of the legal profession has made its mark. For instance, environmental protection laws and consumerism laws might be worth little more than the paper they are printed on but for the able work of public interest lawyers.

From the standpoint of employee rights and constitutionalism, the approach of the public interest lawyer has an outstanding advantage: willingness to settle out of court. Once we have broad guidelines from the courts as to what is and what is not permissible, it will be quickly apparent in most cases whether a complaint of abusive discharge is justified. If it is, the company or agency will have a strong incentive to settle. Damages will be reduced, poor publicity for the organization will be reduced, and, perhaps best of all, some suitable way of putting the person to work again can be devised without the company having to worry about the tendentious policies of a commission or judge.

On the other hand, if it appears that the employee is unjustified in his accusation, both the employer and public interest lawyer can take a hard line and, hopefully, discourage him or her from further pursuit.

THE PRINCIPLE OF JUDICIAL INTRUSION

In Chapter 5 we saw that some federal courts have approved disciplinary measures for wayward companies. For example, in 1974 a federal court decided that Mattel, the toy manufacturer, had repeatedly misled its stockholders; therefore, the court ordered that some outside directors be appointed to the company's board and that management committees be established that would oversee activities not theretofore supervised. The court felt that judgments, fines, and injunctions could not solve the problem. *The way the organization operated* had to be changed.

In extreme cases this approach may also be necessary to assure employee constitutionalism. There will be some companies and public agencies that elect compulsively to fight all ex-employees in courts and tribunals rather than to set up internal procedures for protecting rights, such as those described in chapters 10 and 11. Or perhaps they will not consciously elect to default but will be so clumsily managed that they cannot change their ways. For example, the company or agency might appoint ombudspeople who report to the public relations director, instead of to the chief operating officers, forgetting that a staff man lacks the power to operate effectively in this role.

If a court feels that the improper habits of an organization are ingrained, it could intrude on the decision-making process in still another way. It might put the company on "probation." This was done several years ago after ARCO (formerly Atlantic Richfield Oil Company) was caught spilling oil into a Chicago canal. Despairing of the deterrent value of a $500 to $2,500 fine, for the same plant had been previously convicted of a similar violation, the government's lawyers convinced the district court judge to borrow a page from criminal law. If within forty-five days the company did not correct its procedures for preventing leaks, the judge would appoint a probation officer to supervise a change in approach. Unlike the individual wrongdoer, who can be required to visit the probation officer and report every so often, the corporation could not take the "El" to the downtown courthouse; however, the court-appointed probation officer *could visit it*. So this was what Judge James B. Parsons directed.[10]

Similarly, a federal court could put a "corporate repeater" on probation for violating employee rights, directing a management expert or sophisticated attorney to drop in periodically and see how things are going. If the organization also has a committee and/or board members entrusted with overseeing constitutionalism, the probation officer could work closely with those people.

In a large and complex organization full of bad habits, an inspection team might be needed instead of a probation officer. Here the legal precedent is a 1963 case involving the accounting firm of Levanthol, Krekstein, Horwath and Horwath, which had gotten into trouble with the SEC. A federal court ordered the American Institute of Certified Public Accountants to select an inspection team to go inside the firm and report back on how well it was making certain procedural changes requested by the judge.

Judicial intrusion is by no means an obvious answer. As indicated earlier, it is expensive. It offends the philosophies of many conservatives. Also, some powerful judges may wince at the thought of venturing beyond their traditional limits into the domain of managerial decision making, especially if no measures are taken to relieve the excessive case loads that plague some courts. Nor is judicial intrusion a quick answer. The great white whale of despotism can survive more than a few harpoons—aggressive and assiduous pursuit may be necessary. But if the courts persist, this is the approach that can finally win the day.

In the business sector, is nationalization the ultimate solution for offending corporations? In England, France, and other nations, the call for nationalization is a familiar one. On paper, at least, it is appealing—in one stroke, the executive branch can gain control of the corporation and legislate employee rights for all business and public organizations alike. Yet in practice nationalization loses its appeal. For instance, David Tornquist, a leading journalist in the so-called workers' control movement, concludes: "By lumping industrial power in the ministries of state, nationalization does not guarantee or necessarily favor industrial democracy, but indeed gives rise to bureaucratic forces that will resist workers' management and deploy them in formidable order of battle."[11] And John Kenneth Galbraith refers to "the discovery that the larger and more technical of the public bureaucracies—the Air Force, Navy, Atomic Energy Commission—have purposes of their own which can be quite as intransigently pursued as those of General Motors or Exxon. Private bureaucracies rule in their own interest. But so do public bureaucracies. Why exchange one bureaucracy for another?"[12]

NOTES

1. Lawrence E. Blades, "Employment at Will vs. Individual Freedom: On Limiting the Abusive Exercise of Employer Power," *Columbia Law Review* 67(1967): 1414.
2. Blades, 1427.
3. See *Matrix* (Women in Communications, Austin, Texas), Winter 1975-1976, p. 30.
4. "The Corporation and Its Obligations," An Interview with C. Peter McColough, *Harvard Business Review*, May-June 1975, p. 137.
5. Blades, 1432–1433.
6. *New York Times*, November 13, 1971.
7. Blades, 1433.
8. Thomas Ehrlich, "Legal Pollution," *New York Times Magazine*, February 8, 1976, p. 21.
9. See Luther J. Carter, "Looking Beyond Watergate: The Role of Public Interest Law," *Science*, May 1974, p. 546.
10. Christopher D. Stone, *Where the Law Ends* (New York: Harper & Row, 1975), pp. 184–185.
11. David Tornquist, "Workers' Management: The Intrinsic Issues." In *Workers' Control*, edited by Gerry Hunnius, G. David Garson, and John Case (New York: Vintage Books, 1973), p. 390.
12. John Kenneth Galbraith, *Economics and the Public Purpose* (Boston: Houghton Mifflin Co., 1974), p. 277.

PART V

Conclusion

To keep our democracy, there
must be one commandment:
Thou shalt not ration justice.
—Learned Hand

13

OUR THIRD CENTURY:
MORE SPECIES O
OR
MORE CONSTITUTIONALISM?

The real threat to mankind comes not from microbes or Martians but from Species O, according to two sociologists, Dodd H. Bogart and Havens C. Tipps.[1] Species O has been observed for thousands of years but it did not begin multiplying at an alarming rate until a couple of centuries ago. As it proliferated, its characteristics changed. It became more intelligent, more efficient, more resistant to social control. Originally created by man for such purposes as making money and improving government, it developed the capacity, before people knew what was happening, to manipulate and exploit human beings themselves. The sociologists write:

> Soon the balance of control shifted so that man himself became almost completely dependent on Species O. He had to bend himself to the organization rather than the other way around; the former servant emerged as the master.[2]

What is Species O? It is the self-serving organization. It includes corporations, state and federal government agencies, military commands, university administrations, hospitals, churches. It may also be a division or department of a large corporation or agency. Whenever an organization's inertia, needs for survival, traditions, and "culture" dominate at the expense of the individual's reason and conscience, Species O thrives. "Organization above self," the sign that used to be posted in a famous textile mill, is a good statement of Species O mentality. Don't ask questions, just get the job done. "They" know what is right.

Watergate and Equity Funding in the early 1970s, the price-fixing scandals of the early 1960s, Teapot Dome in the 1920s, portions of the Vietnam War effort—these are dramatic examples of the ravages of Species O. It is probably most dangerous, however, as a low-level infection. When it slowly bleeds the individual conscience dry and metastasizes insidiously, it is most difficult to defend against. There are no spectacular firings or purges in the ranks. There are no epic blunders. Under constant and insistent pressure, employees simply give in and conform. They become good "organization people."

How can the individual conscience hope to assert itself against such overwhelming odds? The voices of dissidence seem futile, like Solzhenitsyns hurling angry words at an unmoving Soviet monolith. Exhortations for enlightened management may do some good, especially with the encouragement of a few companies and public agencies as luminous examples. But if Species O is already advanced in an organization, what hope for change is there then?

Actually, even in enlightened organizations there is no safety. A shift in top management can lead to a striking transformation. The U.S. Supreme Court once cautioned that no nation can reasonably expect that "it will always have wise and humane rulers"; the same goes for a corporation, a school system, or a state or federal bureau.

No wonder, therefore, that so many observers are pessimistic. Species O seems destined to win the anti-Nobel prize. There seems to be no good way of turning it back, at least by outside pressure. This is why, in organizational systems as in political and social systems, it is necessary to work from the inside out.

At the beginning of U.S. political constitutionalism, the colonists foresaw that without clear and guaranteed rights of individual expression, conscience, and privacy, there was little reason to believe this nation might not some day slip back into despotism. Many state legislators voted to ratify the Constitution only because Madison and other national leaders assured them that a Bill of Rights would be added when the first Congress met. That was done, and that step became a giant step, enabling the spirit of the Revolution to survive many crises during the following two centuries. The American Revolution has been called the only revolution that did not disappoint its children.

What holds for the federal and state governments holds for the minigovernments of corporations and public agencies. Every now and then a martyr will come along—a Fitzgerald in the Pentagon, a Pickering in a school system. The martyrs change things for a while but they do not stop Species O for long. Quickly it pervades the organizational body again. Here as in the body politic there must be guarantees to protect free thinkers and dissidents when, as sooner or later must happen, the wind turns temporarily against humanism.

Spokesmen of business and government organizations are often heard discussing in Nixonian fashion how best to "sell the American way of life to the American people." They take advice from top public relations authorities on how best to make the public "believe." One wonders if a small voice in the intended audience shouldn't be asking how the people can sell the American way of life to organizations. If individual rights are so important in homes, political meetings, buses, schools, and property disputes, why are they not also important in the organizations where we spend our working lives? More than a third of all Americans are employed by organizations of some sort.

During the first two centuries of U.S. history, the trend was unmistakably to broaden the reach of the Constitution. Universal male suffrage, the abolition of slavery, bargaining rights for unions, female suffrage, the many extensions of due process to people under arrest or surveillance—these and many other events marked the ever-widening application of the Constitution. But the Constitution does not yet penetrate the organizational sector, the still-dark ghetto of American rights. "The corporation, speaking generally," concludes Arthur Selwyn Miller, "has not yet been 'constitutionalized' by the Supreme Court."[3]

Of course, it would be unperceptive and unrealistic to try to apply the Bill of Rights across the board. Companies and public organizations cannot be run like democracies, their officials elected by ballot, their directives subjected to referendum, their day-to-day decisions debated—at least, not if they are also to be efficient. But is it an either-or choice for our minigovernments—democracy or totalitarianism? Time and again in this book we have seen that a middle ground is possible, practical, and practicable. There can be an imperfect justice—indeed, there probably is no other kind in a sizable organization. We can move pragmatically, flexibly, testing as we go.

If an analogy can be borrowed from political history, we can use the model of Whig-Conservatism, championed by such as the English statesman Edmund Burke, U.S. Justice Felix Frankfurter, and scholar Alexander Bickel; we can eschew moralistic liberalism and militant socialism. When rights take root and spread, growth is endogenous, a shoot here, a shoot there, a thickening from the inside. Evolution, not revolution, has been the story of rights in America. Because we are changing a system employees and employers have grown up with, we must not try to do everything at once but be prepared to leave some problems unresolved for further discussion.

What will distinguish the third century of U.S. constitutionalism? One of its hallmarks should be concern for the rights of employees. Although it is true that the United States showed some concern for employees in the second century of constitutionalism, when rights to collective bargaining, equal employment opportunity, good working conditions, and safety were recognized, it was not until near the very end of that second century, with the Supreme Court's *Pickering* decision in 1968 and the efforts of societies and individuals to establish employee rights, that the country began to focus seriously on the everyday freedoms of most employees—after they begin regular employment, after physical working conditions are made acceptable, and whether or not they are unionized.

ONE BRICK SHY OF A FULL LOAD

Few Americans realize how nearly ready to roll the employee rights wagon is. In 1968 and succeeding years the *Pickering* line of cases introduced the right of free speech into certain public organizations. The implications of this tradition-shattering sequence of cases have scarcely dawned on most people, including employees.

More recently, the Supreme Court of Pennsylvania came within one justice's vote of rendering a decision that would have staggered most corporate lawyers and top managements. The case involved a familiar type of "boat rocking." George B. Geary, a salesman of fourteen years for U.S. Steel Corporation, believed that a new company product, a tubular casing designed for use under high pressure, had been inadequately tested and was potentially dangerous to users. After voicing his misgivings to his immediate superiors, he was ordered to follow directions. Although he did his duties as instructed and did not upset other employees, Geary continued to challenge the product in company conversations, but to no avail. Finally he went to the vice-president in charge of sales of the product and argued his views. Then he was summarily discharged "without cause or notice."

Chief Justice Jones and three other justices took the company's side and decided that it was within its rights in firing Geary. But what is remarkable is that three justices dissented. Not long ago no dissents would have been heard—a quick 7–0 decision for the company would have been virtually automatic. No more. Filing a dissenting opinion, Justice Samuel J. Roberts minced no words about his vigorous conceptual and philosophical disagreement with the majority:

> I cannot accept the view implicit in the majority's decision that today's jurisprudence is so lacking in awareness and vitality that our judicial process is incapable of affording relief to a responsible employee for an arbitrary and retaliatory discharge from employment. I dissent.[4]

Roberts went on to opine that "strong public policies of this Commonwealth have been offended by Geary's discharge," and he quoted Iowa law dean Lawrence E. Blades to the effect that the classical ideal of freedom of contract between employer and employee was an anachronism. He went on to argue: "When a seemingly-absolute right or the conditions of an existing relationship are contrary to public policy, then a court is obligated to qualify that right in light of current reality."

Here is one of the largest industrial states in the union almost ready to establish a major beachhead for employee rights and constitutionalism. Let one more vote change in a decision like this, in Pennsylvania or another major industrial state, and other state courts are likely to follow suit.

Of course, speech is only one of the rights in our proposed bill. It is such a dynamic right, however, that if it is recognized other rights almost certainly will be pulled along with it.

This is not to say that constitutionalism will grow effortlessly in organizations. Its progress is likely to be as halting and painful as the advance of other civil liberties has been. Witness how long it is taking, after passage of the Fourteenth Amendment, for blacks to achieve equal rights, or how long after the first recognition of labor unions nearly a century ago for collective bargaining to become established. But there are signs of major movement, and this fact alone is historic.

Given this general prognosis for an employees' bill of rights, what effect will there be on organizational efficiency? Will the policies of corporations, federal agencies, school systems, and other minigovernments become more responsive to the public interest? Will there be less harmony? What about the outlook for "democracy" in organizations? How will rights influence the individual?

In considering these five questions, let us look past the early years when constitutionalism is being introduced in an organization, for it is predictable that at first employees will feel uneasy about exercising their new rights. Many employees will stay close to the old rules, even after a full bill of rights takes effect in their organizations.

PLUSES, MINUSES, AND QUARKS

Let us assume that all or most of the rights listed in Chapter 9 come into play and that organizations develop suitable means (such as informal courts, ombudspeople, or expedited arbitration) of enforcing them. What will be the effects?

First is the question of damage to efficiency. Justifiably this possibility horrifies many officials. Business executives are the leading worriers, because the money markets hold them accountable. But businessmen are not the only fearful ones. Especially in sectors where the financial pinch is strong, public agency officials worry about trends that threaten efficiency. Labor union executives join them. So do hospital trustees, town managers, and heads of arts organizations.

The fear is not merely that constitutionalism would be useless from the standpoint of efficiency. It is that the employee rights movement may unwittingly become, for all its good intentions, an unguided missile launched against the U.S. economic and service system. In addition to the countless harassments and paperwork demands already imposed on it, management will have to spend still more hours doc-

umenting performance, preparing justifications for its actions, and listening to complaints. How much can it take?
Even in the hands of its most skillful practitioners, the art of
management may not be all that capacious.

This danger cannot be dismissed. According to Richard E.
Walton:

> The rigorous guarantee of human rights, embraced in the
> term "constitutionalism," often involves a trade-off with strict
> task efficiency. Provisions for due process—the right of appeal
> to an impartial authority and protective rules of evidence—
> introduce constraints on managerial action.
>
> Similarly, managing the creation of goods and distribution
> of services can be greatly complicated by open dissent within
> management that focuses on sensitive areas, such as the safety
> of the company's products, the truthfulness of its ads, the na-
> ture of its endeavors to influence governmental bodies, and
> the morality of its foreign operations.[5]

For many thoughtful people, the threat to efficiency is and
will be the major stumbling block to employee constitutionalism. Are there reasons to discount this fear? I
think there are.

To begin, it should be remembered that constitutionalism
is not an untried approach. No one organization recognizes
all of the items in the bill of rights proposed in Chapter 9.
Yet many organizations in the United States have been recognizing one or more of them. As earlier described, IBM
recognizes the right to privacy; its rules are ambitious and
comprehensive. Xerox, General Electric, Massachusetts Institute of Technology, and other institutions have employed
ombudspeople to protect employees who resist unethical
directives, unfair discrimination, and other inequities. In
quite a few organizations, informal courts and arbitrators
have protected many an employee penalized for a candid
tongue.

The companies, universities, and public agencies that
have taken such steps to protect employee rights have not
suffered. They have prospered. What is more, in Sweden
and Norway, where the employee rights movement has ad-

vanced farther than we recommend in this book, a good many companies have managed to set excellent track records for productivity.[6]

Is it just accident that these results have been obtained? Some experienced managers and careful observers do not think so. Rights of expression, conscience, and privacy are seen as forces that enhance employee pride and reduce boredom in the workplace. It may be exceedingly difficult to trace cause and effect—did increased freedom and participation produce the gain in productivity, or was that gain the result of other steps taken by an intelligent management? Might there have been greater gains in efficiency without the rights? And so forth. Still, it can be concluded that a liberal policy does not put a shackle on an organization. At worst, only a Scotch verdict—not proved—can be rendered on claims that U.S. efficiency will be the price of employee rights.

Here is another way of looking at the question. Suppose we had the power to turn the clock back. We are starting all over again, from scratch, seeking to design the best possible system of business, government, and education in this country. After a few early discussions of goals and approaches, different schools of thought develop over the nature of an ideal system. A national debate is arranged. In turn, the spokesmen of the different schools take center stage.

First, advocates of the Taut Ship approach—extreme control, all-out efficiency, and military discipline—present their case. They show how all organizations will operate like fine machines. Organization leaders will be benevolent but all-powerful. Cooperation and coordination will be precise. A happy breed of Clockwork Man will work for the benefit of consumers, communities, and the public at large.

Opponents of this school come forward. "Yes, this looks wonderful on paper," they say, "but in practice you will breed alienation, and in the end efficiency will suffer."

The Taut Ship believers say, "What's the alternative?" Now the advocates of Utopian Worker Democracy outline their case, emphasizing the wonders of an open, expressive, participative organization. But to this program, too, there is a cogent rebuttal. "That may look good on paper, too," opponents charge, "but in actuality you are going to create big happy factories that can't dill a pickle."

Both rebuttals would be right. Whichever plan we choose, serious drawbacks are present. The wisest course is to seek a balance—to optimize, as the engineers say—keeping in mind that the best balance varies continually with the stage of social and economic development, the maturity of constitutionalism in the public mind, and other such influences. The argument of this book is that, because of the stage and mood of the country today, employee constitutionalism is an idea whose time has come. It is not so radical as worker democracy. But it is a marked advance over traditional employer autocracy.

More than three centuries ago a prescient and insightful scholar named Francis Quarles observed, "No sooner is a temple built to God, but the Devil builds a chapel close by." Both the temples of efficiency and human rights have such chapels within easy sight.

Richard Walton puts the same notion in more conceptual terms as follows:

> It can be hypothesized that situations charcterized by only minimum rights depress productivity as well as quality of working life because of the consequences of insecurity, anxiety, and employee resentment on performance. Beyond some point, however, additional forms and degrees of "constitutionalism" continue to improve quality, but at a price to productivity. At a still higher level of constitutionalism, the marginal effect on quality is zero or negligible.[7]

Now let us consider a second question: Will public and private organizations become more responsive to the public interest? More specifically, will constitutionalism help to check the Species O proclivity to engage in Watergate-type scenarios?

Here the employee rights movement should register clear gains. When organization leaders exercise great power for a long period, some of them become arrogant and impervious.

If employees exercise their-rights, dissent will become a wholesome check on arrogant leaders in the organizations of business, government, and public service, just as it has been a check on political leaders.

The key word in this statement, as some will read it, is the *if*. We know that Americans have made good use of their constitutional rights to resist self-serving leaders in government. But we don't know for sure that Americans will exercise any new rights they may gain as *employees*. "In an organization where you're working under supervision, things are different," a skeptic may argue. "There's not all that much interest in what management is doing. Besides, employees are so specialized that they can't possibly put themselves in the place of the managers."

Although this criticism applies to numerous employees, it does not apply to all. For example, it did not apply to such people as Fitzgerald, Pickering, Rafferty, and Downs in the cases of government agency whistle-blowers, and it did not apply to such as Geary, Holodnak, and Zinman in the corporate cases described.

What is more, the evidence suggests that the *potential* for intelligent concern with an organization's policies and purposes is greater than the legal cases might indicate. Consider Studs Terkel's interviews with employees in all walks of life. The interviews make a good test for this purpose because, so far as we know, Terkel had no interest in bringing out some particular angle of employee opinion. He sought to let employees talk about anything that interested them about their work. Just a brief perusal of *Working*[8] will produce numerous instances of employees seeking to relate themselves, despite specialization, to the broader purposes of their employer organizations. For example:

> I was disdainful of bureaucrats in Washington, who set down rules without ever having been to places where those rules take effect. Red tape. I said I could replace a bureaucrat and conduct a program in relationship to people, not figures. [Steve Carmichael, project coordinator for a public youth service agency.]

When you're dealing with a person's money and investments, you deal with his hopes and ambitions and dreams.—David Reed Glover, member of a Chicago brokerage firm.

In some way, I feel my job's important. Especially when you work with people who are trying to save money. It's gratifying for them when they give you the stuff and you mark in their book and there it is—wow! I've accomplished this. And you say, "I'm glad to see you again. You're really doing well." —Nancy Rogers, twenty-eight-year-old bank teller.

The notion that all or nearly all employees below the leadership level are apathetic, unconcerned, uninterested, tunnel-viewing, passive dependents is a very old and faulty notion. Employee rights could be a significant check on corrupt or irresponsible leadership if only one in fifty or one in a hundred employees were to stand on his or her rights of speech, conscience, privacy, or due process. It is true that some of the activists will be malcontents and crackpots. It is true that others will have their facts wrong. But some will be right, and they will make the whole exercise worthwhile. This is the way with an open society or organization anywhere—a church, a New England town meeting, the U.S. Congress, even a class of students. Out of the response, *and out of policy makers' anticipation of possible responses,* comes the counterthrust that may keep an organization from yawing away from the public interest. Would Lockheed officials have tried to lie to Congressmen about C5A cost overruns if they knew the Fitzgeralds in their midst would "commit the truth"? Would the Mattel and Equity Funding scandals have proceeded so far and long under cover of secrecy if employees in the know had felt freer to raise questions out loud? We don't know for sure but it is a good guess that employee rights would have made a difference.

The third question is: What will happen to the internal harmony of organizations?

At the annual meeting of the American Association for the Advancement of Science in Boston, early in 1976, Dr. Arthur Bueche, vice-president for research of General Electric

Company, warned that scientists who criticized their employers' research policies could upset research as well as do the public a disservice. He noted how difficult it often is "to distinguish between those who are blowing the whistle and those who are just crying wolf." He believed that three GE engineers in California who objected to the company's nuclear energy programs had done the right thing when they resigned in order to argue their beliefs in public.

No realist, even an advocate of employee rights, will discount Bueche's fears completely.[9] If critics and defenders of a questionable management policy are working side by side, swimming in the same water, so to speak; if some employees are engaged in community activities that irritate their bosses; if a worker can refuse to comply with an unethical work directive; if employees are jealously guarding rights to privacy that anger certain managers who are trying to make an investigation—then surely there will be friction and distraction. From the standpoint of short-term harmony, it would indeed be desirable to get rid of the disturbers of the peace. But is the loss of harmony likely to be great? For both practical and philosophical reasons, the answer is no.

The practical reason is that employee suspicions of top management exist in almost all organizations, whatever the rights situation. These suspicions cannot be removed by denying their expression. They are fueled amply from the grapevine and personal observation. The only real question is whether they escape like steam from a teakettle or, because of suppression, build up pressure against the sides.

The Soviet Union may be the showcase example. For all its massive efforts to instill harmony, worker dissidence continues. Incapable of finding expression in strikes, bargaining, or at the polls, this dissidence takes the form of apathy, indifference toward achievement, and callousness toward quality and cost control of goods and services. Soviet experts on production long have noted such symptoms in *Izvestia*, *Pravda*, and other publications.

As for the philosophical rebuttal, it came years ago from John Milton. Though best known to posterity as a poet, his discourse on freedom of the press, delivered to Parliament in 1643, has become a classic analysis. "Where there is much desire to learn, there of necessity will be much arguing, much writing, many opinions," Milton said. And wasn't it vital to the nation to keep alive the desire to learn? He decried the pleas for harmony offered by would-be oppressors. He said:

> For this is not the liberty which we can hope, that no grievance ever should arise in the Commonwealth—that let no man in this world expect; but when complaints are freely heard, deeply considered, and speedily reformed, then is the utmost bound of civil liberty attained that wise men look for.[10]

Milton scoffed at the notion that objectionable thoughts could be removed by banishing talk of them:

> Banish all objects of lust, shut up all youth into the severest discipline that can be exercised in any hermitage, ye can not make them chaste, that came not thither so. . . .[11]

Modernize the style and punctuation a little, and substitute a few terms of modern organization governance for English government, and you have as good arguments as there are for accepting the costs of disharmony.

Now for the fourth question: What would employee rights and constitutionalism mean for democracy?

Rights do *not* mean democracy in the primary senses of that word; that is, government by the people (the first two definitions in Webster's) or majority rule (the third definition). Nor do rights come close to the concept of workers' control as defined by leaders of that movement. For example, the bill of rights earlier proposed is by no means a strategy for "democratizing the workplace" or for giving "the workers . . . responsibility for running the enterprise's operations."[12] Nothing in our bill of rights says anything about voting, co-determination (as in West Germany), or management by consensus.

On the other hand, we are talking about an important secondary feature of democracy, what Webster's calls the "principle of equality of rights . . . and treatment" (fourth definition). For many people, this feature is as important as any.

In a society that makes a show of practicing democratic rites, is it consistent to exclude privacy, conscience, expression, and due process from the numerous minigovernments throughout the land? A great many of these companies and agencies are despotic in the harshest sense of that word. In speeches and publications we may criticize the governments of small nations in Africa and Latin America for their rejection of rights. But the gross national products of some of those nations are no larger than the multi-billion-dollar sales volumes of some U.S. corporations. Is it consistent to criticize one group but not the other?

"Benevolent autocracy," a phrase coined by industrial psychologist Robert N. McMurry, may meet the need in some situations but it is no long-term solution for 85 million or more employees. What is democracy? It is an ideology opposed to silence. It does not require a benevolent ruler who "loves the people." A ruler who fears the people's wrath and weapons is preferable. Democracy entails an uncompromising rejection of oppression and suppression.

Finally, how will organizational bills of rights affect the dignity, integrity, and creativeness of employees? This may be the most important question of all. In the long run, the spirit and *élan vitale* of employees are the "bottom line" of institutional performance.

Here we run into a spectacular inconsistency. Our literature promotes the crucial role of emotional health, belonging, integrity, and dignity for members of organizations. Hundreds of millions of dollars are spent every year on programs to assure these qualities—to enrich jobs, improve communications, develop understanding, and increase confidence and self-esteem. But all the while that these millions are being spent on training materials and fringe benefits, we keep the subject employees stripped of the kinds of rights that our socio-political culture calls essential to human dignity.

The trend toward massive, centralized control has nowhere been so much in evidence as in state and federal government and in industry. As Warren Bennis, president of the University of Cincinnati, once noted, the "Freudian trinity of personality" of bureaucracies has grown allometrically. While the executive or ego function has grown strong and powerful, the id and superego functions—legislative and judicial—have stayed puny by comparison. And so the employee feels powerless, manipulated. Enlightened management helps. Job enrichment and worker participation schemes help; equal employment opportunity helps; unions and associations help; occupational health and safety programs help. Even background music in the office and psychedelic colors on the plant walls help. Yet the organization looms enormous, the individual employee small.

"Is my mind so stunted that I can't speak out when I'm bothered about the ethics and social responsibility of this organization?" the employee in many public agencies and companies may well ask. "Is my judgment so bad that I can't involve myself after hours in community activities of my own choice? Is my moral training so poor that I must follow unquestioningly an order to misrepresent or lie, as if I were Clockwork Man? Is my integrity so insignificant that my phone conversations can be recorded without my knowledge and consent and my files cluttered with hearsay information I cannot correct?"

No one seems to know just how much these feelings affect the enthusiasm, morale, and performance of employees. The forces of control, power, and size may have dwarfed our ability to comprehend them.

Yet we sense that something is missing. We can't describe the height, width, and depth of the void but we feel it. The civil liberties advocate must not claim that increased employee rights are a panacea. However, he knows from experience in many fields that advances in rights have a salubrious effect. And he knows that rights of speech, conscience, and privacy, no matter how scathingly attacked on grounds of practicality, pass that final litmus-paper test of any recommendation: *Is it human?*

WHAT ACTION IS NEEDED?

What can companies, government agencies, universities, and other organizations do to make constitutionalism—that is, a bill of rights plus adequate means of enforcement—a reality in the workplace?

On their own initiative, without any official prods and threats from outside, they can create bills of rights for their employees. They can set up mechanisms for enforcement such as those earlier described—informal courts, arbitration, ombudspeople, employee boards, "hot lines," and other devices already tested and proved by one leading organization or another.

An organization's bill of rights should be in writing. The chief executive's support is critical. For instance, behind IBM's strong stand on employee privacy is the complete support of Frank T. Cary, chairman.

If enough companies and agencies voluntarily take strong steps in this direction, the need will be met with a minimum of legislative and legal bloodshed. Let us hope they do. But the *if* is a big one, and so we must consider other kinds of actions as well.

The state and federal courts can stand the common-law rules of employee rightlessness on their head. The judges can decide, as three of seven justices of the Pennsylvania Supreme Court in effect concluded in the *Geary* case, and as the U.S. Supreme Court Majority did in the *Pickering* case, that the hoary rules of centuries past can no longer be tolerated because of changed conditions and public policy. Only ten years ago this prospect could be dismissed as visionary. But for all of their black robes and rich legal phrases, the justices respond humanly to the same *Zeitgeist* as the populace, and there now may be a strong possibility that the state courts or the federal courts, or perhaps both, will make major new decisions in favor of employee speech, conscience, privacy, due process, and other needed rights.

Of course, decisions by federal courts get the job done faster, since their jurisdiction is greater. For instance, the Supreme Court's *Pickering* decision presumably applies to all public school systems and to at least a few types of other public organizations. On the other hand, the state courts have immediate power to decide questions thrown up by myriad state agencies, which collectively employ around 11 million civilians.

But we must not hope for too much from any court system. Judges cannot legislate; they can only decide one question at a time, and even then only when an employee can get enough help from the American Civil Liberties Union, a trade union, friends, or some other source to fight his case from bench to bench. A decision on the rights of a public school administrator does not necessarily apply to an agency official; and a decision on speech by no means applies to immoral directives or privacy.

Moreover, the state courts may take inconsistent approaches to employee rights. One state might go in a radical and extremely permissive direction, while another might take a reactionary approach. The supreme courts of the fifty states feel no compulsion to lie down together.

Another route to constitutionalism might be for state legislatures to pass laws upholding employee rights, perhaps even requiring companies incorporated in the state to enact bills of rights. It is not too much to hope that some states will move in this way—as we have seen, some already have done so in connection with employee rights to buy products and with wiretapping.

Even clear statements of public policy by state legislatures, with no attempt actually to control behavior in organizations, could be significant. For instance, the legislators might declare that it is in the public interest for employees to be able to speak out with impunity about illegal actions being taken by their organizations, to engage in outside activities of their choice, and/or to have certain basic rights of privacy. Such statements would give many a state court the basis to justify broadening employee rights in judicial interpretations.

A U.S. district court in Missouri said as much in a 1975 case involving a veteran engineering manager of General Motors who was fired for accusing the company of making fraudulent statements to the public about engineering matters. In vain the manager sued GM for wrongful discharge because, in the court's words, "no clear mandate of public policy" had been violated.[13]

However, if the state's public policy is clear, the employee can win an upset victory. Peter Petermann, a business agent of a Teamsters union local, was fired after refusing to commit perjury, as ordered by his boss. He sued for reinstatement. In the trial, the Teamsters union argued that its action was justified because of an employer's traditional prerogatives. Fortunately for Petermann, the state's penal code made it a crime to ask a person to commit perjury. Pegging its decision on this fact, the court denied the employer organization's "generally unlimited right to discharge an employee" and ordered Petermann reinstated.[14]

Unfortunately, many state legislators are close to the heads of state agencies, who may bitterly resist such legislation. Also, many legislators are friendly toward corporations; they want more companies to incorporate in their states. For instance, historically Delaware has been one of the most popular states for businesses to incorporate in; it is exceptionally permissive and has been well rewarded for this policy. The odds are overwhelmingly against a bill of rights such as that proposed in Chapter 9 being made a requirement for companies incorporated in Delaware.

There are several forceful measures that the U.S. Congress could take to further the employee rights movement. For employees of federal agencies, the Senate could begin by passing S. 1210, offered in 1975 by Senator Edward Kennedy. However, since only speech is protected in that proposed statute (and even then, only in connection with disclosure of certain information), Congress has much farther to go. If it goes all the way and legislates bills of rights for employees in federal agencies, the results would be significant. As pointed out earlier, in the U.S. Postal Service alone there are 696,100 employees; in the Veterans Administration, 212,100; in the Department of Health, Education and Welfare, 144,900, in the Treasury Department, nearly 129,000. If these more than a million employees became entitled to constitutionalism, the country would be well on its way.

As for employees of most large companies, Congress could put them under the umbrella of constitutionalism by enacting new statutes. Also, as we saw earlier, Congress could introduce federal chartering of corporations. In order to obtain a federal charter entitling it to engage in interstate commerce or take government contracts, a corporation could be required to enact a bill of rights for its employees and institute suitable means of enforcing the rights.

What about a constitutional amendment? This is the most ambitious proposal. In one giant step, rights could be created for employees of all private and public organizations. This was the course the country took in extending the Bill of Rights to blacks after the Civil War (Fourteenth and Fifteenth Amendments), and suffrage to women after World War I (Nineteenth Amendment). Employee rights would be a particularly fitting subject for a constitutional amendment since they represent a fresh extension of principles in the Bill of Rights.

If a constitutional amendment is proposed, it should be fairly general and flexible so that the courts can interpret, modify, and expand it in response to changing times, as they have done with other amendments. For instance, a constitutional amendment might read as simply as this:

> No public or private organization shall discriminate against
> an employee for criticizing the ethical, moral, or legal policies

and practices of the organization; nor shall any organization discriminate against an employee for engaging in outside activities of his or her choice, or for objecting to a directive that violates common norms of morality.

No organization shall deprive an employee of the enjoyment of reasonable privacy in his or her place of work, and no personal information about employees shall be collected or kept other than that necessary to manage the organization efficiently and to meet legal requirements.

No employee of a public or private organization who alleges in good faith that his or her rights have been violated shall be discharged or penalized without a fair hearing in the employer organization.

Because the constitutional road is so direct and visible, it is likely to catalyze opposition more than any other approach would. But it is also the fairest way to achieve employee rights, and in the end it may prove the most satisfactory for all concerned.

PEOPLE VERSUS THEIR ORGANIZATIONS

American institutions everywhere are getting low marks from the public for credibility and performance. These poor ratings appear in survey after survey. Curiously, organizations have come to be seen as something apart from the people who staff them. Those who work in business, government, and the professions do not denigrate themselves. But organizations have become "they," and individuals have become "we," and so it has become possible to berate private and public organizations as if they were lives unto themselves—Species O, to use the nomenclature earlier mentioned.

This tendency to regard people and organizations as existing on opposite sides of a wall cannot be healthy. Although we lack measurements of its ill effects, it can serve no good purpose because the division is spurious. It is a drain on the spirit. The organization line is more subtle than the Mason-Dixon line, the male suffrage line, and other artificial lines that separated Americans in the past; it is within the person rather than between people, psychological rather than geographical, sexual, or ethnic. However, its subtlety does not reduce its destructiveness.

Why has a division developed between "we" the people and "they" our organizations? Many good explanations might be advanced, and the one offered here is only one, but it is significant. We have seen that a serious value conflict exists between organizational life and private life. From kindergarten through high school, from boy scouts and girl scouts to senior citizens groups, from church meetings to town meetings, we are taught respect for discipline and hard work, yes, but also esteem for individual choice, privacy, the expression of conscience, variety of viewpoint. Liberty is part of the American way, we tell ourselves, and, as James Bryant Conant once said, "Liberty like charity must begin at home."

But when we report to work at the average company, public agency, or large professional firm, we find a big exception. As employees we are now supposed to forget some of the values emphasized at home and in school. We are supposed to leave those esteemed rights outside, like cars in the parking lot. We are supposed to concentrate on discipline and to specialize in know-how, as if such needs could not mix with personal rights. "Every time I passed through those plant gates to go to work," the worker told the senator, "I left America, and my rights as a free man."

It is no wonder, therefore, that we suffer from a kind of national schizophrenia, from a lack of value communication between our organized, institutional lives and our private lives. No matter how well-lighted, well-paying, safe, and efficient, the average plant and office become vaguely repressing and depressing in ways that cannot be explained simply by the unpleasantness of having to get out of bed when the alarm clock rings and go to work on tasks that are not always pleasant.

When we join a company, agency, or firm, we make a contract with it—generally not a written agreement but an unwritten one, what some people call a "psychological" contract. In most organizations this contract reads, "In return for a regular paycheck, you shall be obedient to your superiors." John Dean violated this contract in the White House during the Watergate years. A. Ernest Fitzgerald violated it in the Congressional hearings on the Lockheed C5A. Shirley Zinman violated it in a private employment firm. George Geary violated it in a giant steel corporation.

None of these employees and many others like them rejected the need for hard work. In fact, their dissidence made their work harder. Nor did they reject the ideal of loyalty. However, theirs was a loyalty not alone to a fallible management, when it went astray, but to the organization as an ongoing unit, to society, and of course to themselves as conscientious citizens. They would have added another provision in that psychological contract. It might have read: "You shall feel concerned about the way your organization is serving America."

By "Americanizing" our organizations we may produce no magic increases in productivity and performance, though the experience of the few rights-leading companies suggests that gains will indeed be made. But by erasing a subtle division in our culture which makes us rights-holders at home and in the community but puppets in the plant and office, we could reduce an important cause of ambivalence in our outlook. We could become more whole. The American genius has been to seek to bring the halves together—property-holders and non-property-holders, immigrants and native born, North and South, black and white, male and female, liberals and conservatives. Whenever the effort succeeded, the country as a whole succeeded. It is time to begin erasing the division that afflicts some 85 million people and their families—totalitarianism at work versus freedom in the community.

NOTES

1. Dodd H. Bogart and Havens C. Tipps, "The Threat from Species O," *The Futurist*, April 1973, p. 63.
2. Bogart and Tipps, p. 63.
3. Arthur Selwyn Miller, *The Modern Corporate State* (Westport, Conn.: Greenwood Press, 1976), p. 246.
4. *Geary* v. *U.S. Steel Corporation*, 319 A 2d 174, 180 (1974)
5. Richard E. Walton, "Improving the Quality of Work Life," *Harvard Business Review*, May-June 1974, p. 12.
6. See Nancy Foy and Herman Gadon, "Worker Participation: Contrasts in Three Countries," *Harvard Business Review*, May-June 1976, p. 71.
7. Richard E. Walton, "Quality of Working Life: What Is It?" *Sloan Management Review*, Fall 1973, p. 18.
8. Studs Terkel, *Working* (New York: Pantheon, 1974). The statements quoted come from the following pages: 341 (Carmichael), 332 (Glover), 262 (Rogers).
9. See, for example, Phillip I. Blumberg, "Corporate Responsibility and the Employee's Duty of Loyalty and Obedience: A Preliminary Inquiry," *Oklahoma Law Review*, August 1971, p. 279; reprinted in Dow Votaw and S. Prakash Sethi, *The Corporate Dilemma* (Englewood Cliffs, N.J.: Prentice-Hall, 1973), p. 97.
10. John Milton, *Areopagitica*, in *The Harvard Classics*, edited by Charles W. Eliot (New York: P. F. Collier & Son, 1937), p. 189.
11. Milton, p. 208.
12. Gerry Hunnius, G. David Garson, and John Case, eds., *Workers' Control* (New York: Vintage Books, 1973), p. ix.
13. *Percival* v. *General Motors Corporation*, 400 F. Supp. 1322, 1324 (1975).
14. *Petermann* v. *International Brotherhood of Teamsters*, 344 P. 2d 25, 27 (1959).

INDEX